My Musings and Me

My Musings and Me

Frances Helen Kunzweiler

To Mick + Fran

Don said you might enjoy

Frances

iUniverse, Inc.
New York Lincoln Shanghai

My Musings and Me

iUniverse books may be ordered through booksellers or by contacting:

iUniverse
2021 Pine Lake Road, Suite 100
Lincoln, NE 68512
www.iuniverse.com
1-800-Authors (1-800-288-4677)

ISBN: 978-0-595-43661-3 (pbk)
ISBN: 978-0-595-89158-0 (cloth)
ISBN: 978-0-595-87989-2 (ebk)

Printed in the United States of America

Contents

FOREWORD

Publication of this book fulfills one of my life dreams. I started writing poetry and prose when a young girl attending a one room schoolhouse and have continued composing through the present. Though my years are many numbered, each has been a blessing. My musings cover a multitude of topics, life, love, family, friends, neighbors, faith in God, hope, prayer, joy, sadness, history, travel, space, nature, pets, and more.

I dedicate this book to my late husband, Joe, my son Don, my daughter Rita, my grandchildren Karen, Rick, Tim, Denny and Tricia, and to Sister Pauletta Overbeck, O.P all whose inspiration encouraged me to have my work printed. This first volume contains but a sampling of the hundreds I've authored throughout my lifetime. Although my work has been featured in other publications, the contents of this book are exclusively mine. Future volumes are planned to publish the rest.

To you who read these pages, look forward to happiness as each day dawns; share tomorrow's fun and laughter with someone. And, when the cover is closed maybe they will smile recalling joy, not sorrow.

God bless us one and all,

Frances Helen Kunzweiler

MANKIND

Thank you God one more time
From the mighty hurricane
We prayed for protection
With your help we remain.

Our neighborhood was damaged
Many suffered loss
Leaving pain and heartache
Nothing like your agony on the cross.

I can no longer kneel to pray
You my prayers long will linger
Our Fathers, Hail Marys, Glories
Counted on each finger.

If we knew the reason why
Things happen as they do
Tis faith a wondrous secret
Each day we should renew.

Father Ryan speaking at Saturday Mass
Remember each of you attending
God is here watching over us
His love of mankind never ending.

TWILIGHT

Smell the flowers fragrant
Swaying trees in majesty
Oceans roar when tide is high
Beauty ifs found in all of these.

Twilight comes at eventide
Stars give brilliant light
Full moon casts a golden glow
Preparing us for a morning bright.

Birds on a branch to rest
We use magic concentration
Knowing families will reside
In this world our nation.

There are multitudes of angels
Waiting on gossamer wings
When we stumble they assist
With harps and melodies they sing.

Being a good Samaritan
Any time of year or weather
That should be each day we live
Not when desperation brings us together.

FRIEND

Busy hands
Happy heart
Wondering
Will I finish
Things I start

Write a poem
Hum a tune
Realize all too soon
Message send
To a lonely
Long time friend.

ANYTIME

Say a prayer
Any time no matter
What your doing
It will help you
Concentrate on
A venture you're pursuing.

THINK

Yesterday
Where did it go?
Thoughts a million miles away
Should be on the go
Or find a dress

I started to sew
Think a moment
Yourself to please
Ask God
Put your mind at ease.
Windowsill

When winter comes
Do you suppose
We need gloves, caps, muffs
Or frost bitten toes.

Yet when snow covers the ground
The earth is silent, get the sled
Glide down the hill
Grab icicles from
The windowsill.

Sharpen up the ice skates blade
Enjoy a frozen pond nature made
Waiting for all to try
Something we called, The Butterfly.

Make snow men, decorate
Coal for eyes, carrot nose
Pink bubble gum for lips
Small wooden chips for toes.

Use dad's old hat and vest
A small green branch, by mom's request
Growing up in the country
Golly gee, way back when
Life was really worry free.

PAPER BAND

Thoughts I had this morning
Memories come to mind
Pleasure an understatement
Written back in olden time.

Joseph K gave to me
A paper band for my finger
Think of this a little while
Before answering, thoughts linger.

Holidays were coming
Halloween, Thanksgiving, Christmas too
Told me he would replace the paper band
December fifteen, nineteen thirty-two.

For me a band of diamonds
Much to my surprise
Asking me to marry him
Tears came to my eyes.

Results were a wedding
In Peoria way back when
Pastor Father Tom Gaulmann
Saw the little paper band.

A surprise the question asked
His voice was a command
My answer, "my engagement ring"
A cigar golden paper band.

DON

When I am gone do not be lonely
You have been a wonderful son
Toiling in home and garden
Until setting of the sun.

You must take time enjoying life
Time passes quickly this I know
Doing for others gives enjoyment
Memories will ever flow.

Ne'er let anyone abuse you
Always be a friend
Travel many places you desire
Money is to use and spend.

Having enjoyed years I've lived
Until age and feet begin to slow
Let not your life be burdened
Times passes, sometime tears overflow.

Have what you want, see the world
Maybe a condo by the sea
Don't skimp and save, enjoy, enjoy
You did everything for me.

Love, Mom

STEPS

A monument of granite and marble
Located in Washington, D.C.
Words engraved
Laus Deo for all to see.

Eight hundred ninety steps
To the top, fifty places
You may rest
These two words in Latin
Ask, answer "Praise be to God"
Given on request.

Signs placed there
Many years we sigh
555 feet, 6660 inches high
Looking out viewing sights
You can almost reach the sky.

White House to the north
Jefferson Memorial South
Lincoln Memorial on the West
Capitol of our nation the East
We saved that for the best.

Construction lasted twenty-five years
Millions of visitors give a nod
Look up and enjoy these structures
"*Laus Deo*", Praise be to God.

JOURNEY

Remember on vacation
Time, thoughts will stray
Whether overseas or close to home
For journey memories sing a song.

Of places visited in years past
All meant very much
England, Ireland, Scotland, Wales
The Swiss Alps were a must.

A million miles were traveled
Views of Big Ben, Venice, and Milan
The people loved entertaining us
Back then our USA was a foreign land.

Now at ninety years of age
Looking at poetry on every page
Memories of importance
Found on a yellowed page.

Keep loved ones daily informed
Places visited mean a lot
Some may never have a chance
To visit *Camelot.*

Words bring joy to many
Some might shed a tear
Their thoughts will be comfort
On your journey next year.

AUTUMN

There is music found
In watering flowers
Butterflies, honey bees, birds
Enjoy the sprinklers showers.

When the wind starts blowing
Scatters leaves everywhere
Air is getting chilly
Autumn is in the air.

Soon mums will be blooming
Colors rust, red and gold
Squirrels hiding acorns
For food when winter cold.

Take the seasons all in stride
Thanksgiving Day is near
Soon we decorate for Christmas
A joyous time of year.

THE PIER

Going to dinner one night
We picked a place called *Crabby Joe's*
Located in the Sun Glow Pier
Some place my daughter chose.

Reaching into the ocean
Many folks were there to see
Shrimp boats returning with their catch
Brought memories to me.

The Alps in Switzerland were marvelous
Also the Danube Blue
Ocean liners on the sea
A lasting memory to view.

Having been to Texas
All the states out west
I fell in love with the Emerald Isle
Scotland, Italy, Wales
The entertainment was the best.

After fourteen days seeing sights
I would like for all to know
The sights you enjoy from Sun Glow Pier
Leave memories that overflow.

GAMES

Did you ever pick
A Dandelion when dry
Make wish, blow gently
Petals start floating to the sky.

Pick petals from a daisy
Say he loves me, loves me not
Here each came out in favor
"He loves me", loves me not.

Play a game of Dominos
Stand them in a line
Then your goofy brother
Sneaks up from behind.

Saying, Sis I'm sorry
I'll make it up to you
First I have to bat some balls
To Chuck, Tom, Norv, Russ and Lou.

Games were played, friends were made
On farms where we all lived
Memories linger, take me back
Our motto, *Forget—Forgive.*

FAITH

Did you ever stop
Seeing birds in flight
How many times their wings flap
When landing in a tree to nap.

Hear the ripple of a stream
Racing o'er the stones
Maybe bring some pleasure
At the farm of Mister Jones.

May the golden moon when shining
Be a beacon, light the way
For a lonesome traveler
Waiting for the light of day.

Soon the sun in heaven glistens
Things of earth thrive, this I know
Wind blows, rain falls, flowers bloom
Birds fly in formation, putting on a show.

We must never question
The magic found everyday
Because the Master's creation
Faith will help a long the way.

TIME

Time to live
Time to love
Time to thank
The stars above
Time to laugh
Time to cry
Time to happy be
Do something for someone
An act of Charity.

Time to listen
Time to learn
Time to show
Real concern.

Time to help
Someone in need
It's not a pity
Just generosity.

Time to raise
Your voice in song
Time to show
Them they belong.

Time will come
When they feel great
Then it is time
To celebrate.

ABCs

A—Always be happy

B—Because you show

C—Caring for others

D—Dear people you know

E—Each time you held someone

F—Fun and happiness you show

G—Give a call, help a friend

H—Hoping to give pleasure

I—Imagine what life would be

J—Joy will be a treasure

K—Knowledge we share is free

L—Love received generously

M—Million thoughts we give

N—Never let the day be ended

O—Others need to forget and forgive

P—Prayers needed and extended

Q—Questions asked with a smile

R—Rest sometimes is worthwhile

S—Suggestions make life inspiring

T—Treasures found, doing, trying

U—Using energy expectations

V—Volumes leave time for caring

W—Waiting, watching no obligations

X—Xtra satisfaction sharing

Y—Yonder years gone I confess

Z—Zoom in celebration, be my guest.

EARTH

Did you ever watch a gentle rain
Drop on each leaf, petal and ground
Glistening like a million diamonds
It was quiet all around.

Soon a brilliant sun like magic
Caused them to dry right away
They went down to nourish earth
Things happen, why we pray.

All God's blessings we receive
Sun, moon, wind, stars
Green forests; modern highways,
Carry many million cars.

So if every you feel lonely
Need a chance to add some mirth
Just look around you will find
Life is great on mother earth.

MY LIFE

Time to write my story
Born Lee Summit, Missouri, July 20, 1914, golly gee,
A large family, ten with father and mother
Having wonderful times playfully.

Frieda, Louise, I was third in line
Followed by five brothers
There were times I felt neglected
Doing for all the others.

Charles, Tom, Norv, Russell, Bob
I like to follow them around
It was a chance I had to take
Because they'd tease me with a snake.

School was held in one large room
All eight grades were together
When anyone misbehaved
A strap used was made of leather.

Our work was laid out for each
Before class and after school
Reading, writing, arithmetic
Also taught the Golden Rule.

Pupils came from miles around
Hours were nine to four
Difficult times always found
Needy families, some quite poor.

[MY LIFE—continued]

A big stove in one corner
Used corncobs, wood and coal
The winter months seemed endless
Diseases took their toll.

I graduated when eleven
Taking two years in one
A student of Yatesville school
Learning to me was fun.

Jacksonville, Illinois the county seat
We took our eight grade test
Graduated ninth of three hundred forty three
I did my very best.

Doing housework for people
When I was age thirteen
Laundry, ironing, scrubbing floors
Left little time to dream.

Married when age eighteen
To a wonderful guy named Joe
Moving to Springfield, Illinois
The best man I will ever know.

The year was nineteen thirty-two
Dances, parties, conventions
Wanting to have a family
Was our best intention.

[MY LIFE—continued]

December six, nineteen thirty-four
Our son Donald Joseph, "D.J."
A multitude of auburn curls
Pleasure filled our life each day.

Then in nineteen thirty-seven
October twelve the date
Daughter Rheta Louise was born
We sure had reason to celebrate.

Through the years grandchildren came
My years with Joe too few
Angels took him to live with God
In January, nineteen seventy-two.

Karen, Rick, Tim, Denny, Tricia
Each began at St. Patrick's in Springfield
Later the family moved to Daytona Beach
Though still in Illinois, I kept close reach.

Great grandchildren number four
Stephanie, Chelsea, Callahan, Joe
That's enough I do believe
Never quiet, always on the go.

One great-great grandson Chase
Comes to visit once in a while
He isn't crazy about Schnauzer Jacques
But his cat Sylvester makes him smile.

Years have passed quickly
Many things I've seen and done

[MY LIFE—continued]

Traveling miles by air, ship, train, car
Enjoying every one.

July twenty, 2004 I celebrated
Ninety years on earth
The greatest place I know
USA the country of my birth.

Remember these who read this
Enjoy life each day you live
If someone hurts you in any way
Learn to forget, forgive.

My last request, love I leave
Have a Mass, maybe some will come
If not my angel will be there
Say a prayer, well done.

Faith I leave with everyone
As on this earth you trod
Say your prayers, remember
Your life is lost without God.

Love,

Mom

GOLDEN YEARS

As children we dream about things
Growing up what to do
Teenagers make conversation
Their troubles very few

Young people think the golden years
Are when fifty or more
Were I to return to golden years
It would be ten plus four.

Adult age brave challenge
Future all shiny and bright
Then realize with great surprise
Teenage years were sheer delight.

Golden years those without fears
Not when you hair turns gray
Golden eight to eighteen years
Live, enjoy them each day.

Being in the olden years
With loving people who care
If ever you need someone's help
Ninety years I'm willing to share.

I believe the great happiness man can give
Helping one less fortunate to live.

HIS SKILL

The snow lays heavy on the ground
Cold winters give me a chill
If wondering why all this must be
The Master has shown his skill.

He shrouds each branch with beauty rare,
Then shines the sun in glory
Glistening icicles are everywhere,
It's like a fairy story.

As a child I walked to school
On snow above fence tops high
With no modern conveniences
Still we managed to get by.

I guess I'm still a kid at heart
'cause when the winter comes
I hope it snows to fill the earth
So please don't feel glum.

No artist does what God can do
The skill that He can show
He makes the rain and rivers
And trees that grow and grow.

I love every earthly thing
And people who life on it
No one could do a better job
But I can write a sonnet.

OFFERING

Thanks and prayers are offered
For people I call friend
Especially Sister Pauletta Overbeck
Who created a cover to send
Along with poems I have written
Should they ever be a success
One to be given credit
Should not be hard to guess.

A Master who guides a willing hand
A Springfield Dominican nun
My son Don who daily puts up with me
From day to set of sun.

May I pass out praises
To each a bouquet of love
They all have many talents
Keeping stars shining above.

Thanks again beautiful people
May the pathway you trod
Be strewn with choicest blessings
Let by the hand of God.

A TRIBUTE

I went to a school, not sent there by force
To enjoy life more fully, from a well chartered course
In walking, standing or sitting, these lessons will guide
If you follow the pink book and do so with pride.

One instructor, Miss Florence, I know you recall
Was so very gracious with kindness for all
Frances Pound with her brogue must have come from the south
As she speaks her eyes twinkle, a smile frames her mouth.

Mary Sedekum gets attention when she takes the stand
Dorothea Doetsch with a gleaming diamond on her left hand
All these instructors are very sincere
They drive quite a distance to teach us up here.

We have nurses, secretaries, housewives too
A piano teacher, bookkeeper, toy counselor oooh
Could we get a discount Irene, if we tried
Or money from Wilma Steidley's bank on the side.

We may see Alice Meier for a dinner by jove
Or see Mary Alice for a fancy new stove
Say Vickie, could you teach me the do-re-mi
We might ask Lois Watson if federal housing is free.

To Ruth Sprinkel for gravel or a yard full of sand
Mary Aleshire could nurse us, there's a person real grand
Buelah Crouch a housewife, now what could be better
Unless we drove to Taylorville to visit Shirley Etter.

[A TRIBUTE—continued]

JoAnn Calandrino a secretary works for our state
Fran Harms a keen housewife makes employers wait
If our car needs some oil to Barb Huddelston we'll go
Then drive to South College and visit Paula Pidcoe.

Wilma Davidson another housewife, so tiny and sprite
Norma Blue a nurse, call her day or night
The entire class roster I've enjoyed everyone
Especially the visit to Ruth's new little home.

It can't be just six years, won't you all agree
That spit curls were popular, I would be just twenty-three
Come on Mrs. Ryder, if this is the truth
You must have been drinking from the Fountain of Youth.

I feel the progress I made will last all my life.
Being interested in learning, heeding some sound advice
I'll try to grow as through life I go
Share the knowledge gained, keep my memories aglow.

Here's to all my acquaintances I met at this school
The best life has to offer, a valuable rule.
Those lessons so helpful they taught us to smile
With sincerity, honesty, genuine style
These were great weeks of action packed fun you will see
I let Dorothy Carnegie help me to be happy and carefree.

BEAUTIFUL PEOPLE

Thanking God each day for living
In this country without restriction
Beautiful people like Joan, Charlie, Margot, Ernie, Heather
Can make it a great benediction.

Our land of promise for everyone
Especially enjoying neighbors and friends
Its good to be having pace of mind
From days beginning to end.

Most beauty comes from deep within
Shared in visiting, fun and laughter
Why keep searching everywhere
Its understanding we are after.

Kindness shown the past few years
With just the wave of a hand
Helped erase many lonely hours
Seems they could understand.

So my thanks are offered
With feelings from the heart
Gracious kindness you have shown
Leaves memories to impart.

To each of you the best in life
Enjoy pleasures till they overflow
And I shall greet up and down the street
The most beautiful people I know.

TOMORROW

Many miles many travels
In our life on earth
Why! A question often asked
My answer, smiles and mirth.

Greetings from a stranger
Or wave from a child's hand
Burdens can be lifted
Like the surf on oceans sand.

Look around see the beauty
That surrounds us everywhere
Brings pleasure not a duty
Thoughts of comfort not despair.

View leaves changing color
When they turn from green to red
Hoping all will be forgiven
Something we might have said.

So when I close my eyes at night
Feeling sleep will bring no sorrow
My angel will give me a chance
To enjoy a better day tomorrow.

THINK

A good days beginning
The happy days end
Mixed with some pleasure
In a prayer. Amen.

Thank the Lord and master
Traveling along the road
No need to see what lies ahead
My angel helps carry the load.

Think of the road we traveled
And steps your feet have trod
None of these were possible
Without the grace of God.

Why worry about tomorrow
Live today as best you can
Someone may be lonely
A message by phone would be grand.

Go on, send them a greeting
Tell a joke to make them smile
It will be worth the effort
When you walk that extra mile.

THE REVERENDS

Two very educated priests
Of the human race
Caused misunderstandings
The congregation had to face.

We do not know the reason
Too gracious to ask why
Could problems have been settled
Had they given it a try.

When little children get tangled up
Fail to get along with each other
Parents tell them, work it out
You're supposed to love your brother.

You know the one who is the boss
Let evil feelings overflow
Forget, forgive those little ills
Let not anger show.

As a convert with age of eighty-nine
I have seen many come and go
Tis like the old-old saying
It takes two to tango.

Now listen guys and realize
You maybe had a misunderstanding
But every flight that takes off
Needs to have a happy landing.

THE GUARDIAN

There is a guardian angel
Assigned to you and I
Although we never see them
Protecting us, need not ask why.

Their voice may be a whisper
That tells us what to do
Comes when there is danger
Yet we do not have a clue.

I know someone is ever watching
In an hour of need
And vanish before we thank them
For doing a good deed.

Yes I believe in guardian angels
As on this earth we trod
They are on a mission
As a messenger of God.

SIS

Sis, I like the items you write about
Printed in the Ashland paper
Keeping your mind occupied
Gives no time for foolish caper.

When happiness fills your days
Whether tending flowers or dusting
If you worry about tomorrow
The thoughts could be disgusting.

Bake a cake, grill a steak
When the sun sinks in the west
You have made your life worthwhile
When you settle down to rest.

Wish you could come and visit
About family, friends, memories glow
Things we did at Yatesville school
That happened so many years ago.

Take care of Jim, and Rich's family
Also yourself; you've stood the test
Many things happen in our lives
What we don't like, we put to rest.

REMEMBERING

Sure I remember Prentice
And Mr. Felix' grocery store
The candy jar was always open
You could take one piece not any more.

Graduating from Yatesville School
When only twelve years old
There was just one in the class
Those remaining did not pass.

Working in Springfield, Illinois
The summer I was thirteen
Making three whole dollars a week
Was like living in a dream.

My mom would pick me up in Ashland
Going to the country we would stop
Holbrooks ran the grocery store
We would buy a five-cent soda pop.

Charlie and Bertha ran the market
There was a Smithy and elevator
M<y father used to work there
Carl Weakley was boss administrator.

Charlie drove the grocery truck
Through the country twice a week
Mom sold him eggs and chickens
We kids all got a treat.

[REMEMBERING—continued]

Those days gone not forgotten
Of all the families we knew
Hendersons, Donovans, Stice, Sommers, Freitag
Bloomfield, Lambkulars, Ora Mae Wood
Just to name a few.

There was one named Ed Cashin
Thought he was quite a man
Used to torment my brothers
Six of us were Edwards clan.

The memories I have gathered
Will not ever fade away
Our world in all its changes
The progress that's been made.

Having seen many gone, not forgotten
In my years of eighty-nine
Though footsteps are getting slower
Life to me is mighty fine.

PARENTS

Our father and mother taught us
Be honest love one another
Eight children in our family
Three sisters and five brothers.

Many times it was not easy
Frieda, Louise, Frances also known as Ann
Charles, Thomas, Norval Russell
The youngest Robert end of the clan.

All attended Yatesville school
Eight grades in one big room
Learning reading, writing and arithmetic
Days ended all too soon.

Teachers Gruber, Lonergan and Puhl
Taught grammar and spelling and how to act
Had to recite the ABCs backwards
Was used as a matter of tact.

The memories still linger
An acre of land where we used to play
The in-ground well we used to prime
For cool water to drink each day

Climbing the old cottonwood tree
Carry in coal and wood to keep us warm
Close the wooden shutters from the storms
So broken glass would not cause students harm.

Like all things through the years
As old books worn out pages

Memories will ne'er be forgotten
Regardless of time and ages.

AN ANGEL CAME TO GREET HIM

On March ten two thousand and three
The Lord held out his hand
An angel was there with Norval
This I believe and understand.

Dear God you took another brother
I loved them all so very much
Accept him in your heavenly kingdom
With dad, mom, sisters and brothers
So all may keep in touch.

We had a letter from you three days ago
On Sunday a long phone call
About how our steps are getting slower
And the future for us all.

Wanting to get together
Sharing laughter having fun
Not knowing days were numbered
At the rising of another sun.

Norval was a joy for all
With such a happy smile
Being great at conversations
Helped make living so worthwhile.

Please God our Lord and Master
Keep our love for you carefree
There is no doubt you care for all
Until we enter eternity.

Watch over Maureen, Tom and Terry
And their families one and all
Let us keep in touch quite often
By e-mail, letter or phone call.

Now I say a prayer for Mary
She has carried quite a cross
Please don't forget her angels
Help her carry her heavy loss.

OFF TO THE EMERALD ISLE

Members of St. Paul Parish Choir
Are off to the Emerald Isle
Know they will be greeted
With a shamrock and a smile
Departure date is sixteen October
Here's wishing you the very best
And praying everyone stays sober.

There are many things to see and do
When you reach Killarney
They have no snakes to scare you
As you climb to kiss the blarney
There is Johanna, Pat, Marie, Rose, Tom and Tom
Fr. Ralph, Roy, Bob, Annette Mary Ellen and Don
Sing out so your songs are full of joy
Just like in a marathon.

Robin, Irene, David, Bill, Susan, Betty Jane, Dolores
When singing people might ask to join in the chorus
Have some fun along the way
And while visiting some Irish pubs
Hope you tip up one to me
Maybe enjoying a Guinness suds.

Time passes very quickly
Join in the laughter and be merry
If you're all thumbs you won't have fun
Especially on the Ring of Kerry
Having overheard people in church
Visiting Ireland would be a dream

My trip there years ago was great
Even drinking Irish Cream.

So gals and guys have a great time
You may get tired and weary
Remember what happened years ago
To Chicago's Maggie O'Leary
May your memories all be pleasant
As you start your trip back home
Remember no fools—no fun for anyone
Put complaints out on a loan.

MIXTURE

Yes, I'm a little English

Oh, a wee bit Irish too

In between there is some German

With a pinch of French, adieu

And yet a real American

A Yankee from the heart

Living in a mixed up country

Where our freedom is a part

Of facing each day happier

With peace in this great land

Hoping in the future

We strive to walk hand in hand.

JACQUES

Storm clouds seem to gather
Late afternoon around four
Lightning strikes comes the thunder
With a loud tempest roar.

Jacques does not like this noise
Created by a thunderous blast
If he could talk he would say
How long will this stuff last.

He is a special Schnauzer
From storms he tries to hide
Wondering when this rain stops
Maybe I will get a ride.

Each morning around seven
He is ready for a walk
All around the neighborhood
To see other folks, stop and talk.

We meet all kinds shapes and sizes
When we take our evening stroll
But come back home in a hurry
When the thunder starts to roll

INSPIRATION

Think about the words you see
As news each day you read
There is please in pleasure
Act in action to succeed

Cat tear and great in category
Song and sing in something to
Why worry it causes wrinkles
Ink in this last word is blue.

Cut is found in lettuce
Motto, at in tomato too
Tattoo is in potato
And aid is in adieu.

Saw-say are in sway
Sin and wing in Swing
Reign and rig in Ginger
Also gin and grin in your ring.

Speculation has elation
Prosperity has pity trip, and try
Anticipation has a station
Ever in never do not ask why.

COURAGE

I wonder may I be of service
It could do no harm
Visiting a friendly neighbor
Ideas and thoughts to add charm.

Should they travel through the country
As the leaves turn red and gold
Discover new found happiness
Perhaps memories might unfold.

Whispering winds so gently blowing
Azure blue of sky above
Rippling water in the streams
Seen nearby a turtle dove.

Pick up a rock to treasure
As daylight begins to fade
Have a thought of profound pleasure
And courage do not be afraid.

If I have helped in any way
A reminder is worthwhile
Come and visit anytime
Welcome mats here are in style.

FULL MEASURE

There's a mile in every smile
An ounce in every pound
A drop in every rainfall
And a song in every sound.

A pint in each gallon
A plant from each tiny seed
You find ill in every pill
Success is needed to succeed.

A grain of salt may be found
In each Morton's box you open
A ray hope to someone lonely
When gentle words are spoken

There is life in living
Having memories to treasure
Share some happiness today
Filling the cup to fullest measure.

Oft times we stop to wonder
What the future may have in store
Send cards of cheer thru the year
That's what good friends are for.

FAMILY

Rumble of thunder symbol of rain
Lightning threads of silvery white
Earth needs moisture so things will grow
Filling hearts with delight.

We were all happy as youngsters
Greeting everyone with smiles
My memories return to being young
Time past would measure in miles

Charley and Lottie were the parents
Sisters Frieda, Louise, they called me Ann
Charles Jr, Thomas B, Norval Leo
Russell Sherwood, Robert Eugene formed our clan.

Down through the years as we grew up
Midst happiness tears and laughter
The old country school we attended
Left lingering thoughts ever after.

Years have passed sadness came
Charley and Lottie called to God
Missing them as all were young
Then Russell their pathway trod.

Scattered about as large families are
Trying to keep close cross the miles
Then you called
Tom, a joy to all
His love for mankind wreathed in smiles.

[FAMILY—continued]

Charles was slim and tall
He had a steady hand
Toiled and worked everyday
To keep up with demand.

Each in their way loved you Lord
Give us strength to pray
Understanding the reason
Taking our loved ones away.

Lost and lonely without your help
We stretch out our hand
Like the rumble of thunder you give us
Life to view lightning's silver strand.

Louise was the next to follow
She was ready, answered your call
To meet the others at rest
Frieda the oldest soon would fall.

We knew it was God's request
On March ten of twenty-o-three
You took Norval to be your eternal guest
A beacon of hope to rely on, important was your request.

Many other family members were taken
Joe was one of the best and genuine
There never could be another
He was really one of a kind

[FAMILY—continued]

Ray Scott and his son Jerry
Marion Shaw, Carl Orne and Dorothy
Margaret, then Mary
Many times I got lonesome
You give me strength to grow
To pray, live life each day
As footsteps are getting slow.

Now Bob has joined the departed
The last brother to answer your call
Keep them close in your kingdom
While memories of each we recall.

On January twenty three twenty-0-four
The last son of mom and dad's clan
Bob was a companion for a year in Florida
When called he answered your command.

DAYS

Monday
> A day spent first of the week
> And when over, you feel some squeak.

Tuesday
> Do not get angry try and be merry
> Then the burden won't make you contrary.

Wednesday
> The middle of the week can you believe
> Better get busy there is much to achieve.

Thursday
> Sort of a ho-hum day
> Walk around trouble in your way.

Friday
> Workers are happy it is T.G.I.F.
> Think of others while traveling, not yourself.

Saturday
> A day for cleaning, baking, all that good stuff
> Make the most of it when going gets rough.

Sunday
> With sun this day may you find
> Happiness always the very best kind.

CARE

Little deeds like little seeds
Grow, grow and grow
Some bring flowers some are weeds
Spreading joy or woe.
So try planting happiness
Everywhere you go.

Among the beautiful memories
Of years past eighty and more
Finding myself enjoying life
There are things to explore.

Traveling again on vacation
O'er oceans where hidden life play
Yet meeting someone for luncheon
Will brighten a gloomy day.

Take time to visit a shut-in
Wish them all is well
A greeting card with message
An idea on which they may dwell.

Care how others are feeling
May they have memories that grow
With treasures of understanding
Adding prayers help, this I know.

A WEEK

Monday starts each week for me
I think what should I do
But I must not tarry very long
Since Tuesday will be due.

So now it's Wednesday, the middle day
Gee the week is halfway gone
So I better not be idle
As Thursday is rushing right along.

With Friday comes T.G.I.F.
Better clean the house and mop the floor
Saturday is here already
Time to bake, shop at the store.

Sunday is a day of pleasure
Go to church and share a smile
You will find all your efforts
Help make living so worthwhile.

A NEW DAY

Start each day with a smile
Even though you might feel sad.
The sun shines in, dispels the gray
Then you won't feel so bad.

Have yourself a cup of coffee
Or whatever drink you choose
Putter around with little duties
What have you got to lose.

Get in the car, do some shopping
Go to the dollar store
Say hello to someone you meet
Feel better, why ask for more.

And when the sun is setting
As daylight starts to fade
Feel secure and never have doubt
For the progress you have made.

A MINUTE

Share your light
With those around you
Brighten a cloudy day
Hum a tune of happiness
Give your mind a chance to stray.

When today becomes tomorrow
Yesterday was here a minute
Leaving me no thoughts of sorrow
Cause I put my efforts in it.

Remembering things I hold dearly
Always wishing you were here
Linger just a little longer if someone proposes
Take a moment stop and pause
Smell the fragrance of the roses.

I know there is work to do
There really is not a limit
Relax unwind, you will find
It only takes a minute.

ANGELS

I saw a little girl alone
Asking may I help, she said I have no home
Tears came quickly to my eyes
As she stood by my side
We started walking slowly
She said many times I cried.

Looking at her tear stained face
She said may I live with you
I will be good I promise
May I bring my dolly too.

I questioned how old are you darling
Her answer I do not really know
They told me we have no room for you
So you will have to go.

Opening the door very wide
Closing it after me
Dark at night and very cold
I could hardly see

Being tired I just sat down
Then you found me there
Whispering very softly
At last someone will care

Can I go with you, share my life
From you I will not roam
Angels prayed, softly said
We found this child a home.

GREAT GRANDCHILDREN

Moving to the sunshine state
In nineteen hundred ninety-five
Away from ice and snow in Illinois
So happy to arrive.

Building a home to treasure
Sharing happiness and joys
When great grandchildren come to visit
They number four
Two girls and two boys.

Stephanie the oldest
Age of twelve
Then Chelsea who is eight
Along came Joe and Cal
To them life is great.

Talking, laughing having fun
Baseball, fishing, CDs, going places
Skateboards, bikes and roller blades
They end the day with smiling faces.

How rapidly they grow up
Too busy all the time
Will they have memories
Asking this is *out of line.*

THOUGHTS AND WORDS

Think of things that make you happy
Why sit and wear a frown
Look for <u>fun</u> in funny
Be goofy as a clown.

Did and dog are found in <u>doing</u>
Also a car and race in <u>care</u>
A flaw and law in <u>awful</u>
Raw-bar-bee-bear-war in <u>beware</u>.

There is leap and ape in <u>apple</u>
<u>Reap</u> has an ear, pea and pear
Money and key are in a <u>monkey</u>
<u>Season</u> has a son-nose and sea.

In <u>holiday</u> you find lady-hold-hay-hi and ho
<u>Knowledge</u> has edge-wedge-ledge-now and know
Action-race-ran-lion-trace-brace in <u>celebration</u>
Rail-tail-bat-bit-tub in <u>jubilation</u>.

<u>Imagination</u> a man-giant-gain-tag-nag and gin
<u>Contemplation</u> a cat-tail-mail-man and nation
There a panic-cat-ant-paint in <u>anticipation</u>
You will find a tonic in <u>consolation</u>.

GRANDCHILDREN

Our family grew from four to seven
When four were married it was number eleven
Lo and behold what came on the scene
Two great-granddaughters add up to thirteen.

An unlucky number many might say
The pleasure they bring makes living okay
Stephanie the oldest, then Chelsea blond and petite
Watching them grow a wondrous treat.

Two years passed then came two more
Great-grandsons this time now total of four
With open arms we welcomed them here
Joey and Callahan precious and dear.

Opening hearts, willing to explore
Love them so much and if there are more
Give them courage, the strength they will need
Later in life hoping each will succeed.

Growing up a struggle, all is worthwhile
Seeing them together is reason to smile
Problems forgotten at the time of birth
Because they live in the greatest country on earth.

JOY

See the azure blue of the sky
Shown in all its splendor
A cardinal in a distant tree
Whistling to its mate
Getting a shower from sprinklers
Down by the garden gate.

Jade green lawn in early morn
Plants blooming brilliant red
Bird baths filled with seedlings
Where birds are daily fed.

Stroll along the garden path
A stone bench will beckon
Squirrels jump from tree to tree
Which only takes a second.

The blessed statue of Our Lady
Seems to nod her head
While Saint Francis and Saint Joseph
Stand nearby in the flower bed.

Soon the sun was brightly shining
No cloud was in the sky
A gentle breeze was blowing
Children fishing in the lake close by.

REMEMBER

The glory of Autumn
Its magic divine
Whistles of red cardinals
In three quarter time.

Rumbling of thunder
And lightning's gleaming strike
Rain pours down in torrents
Drenching everything in sight.

Suddenly the sun is shining
From sky of heavenly blue
Tis wonders of God's creation
Our faith is tried and true.

So when you feel great sadness
For our loved ones gone away
A reason we might be our best
Enjoy life, love, appreciate each day.

Let's say a prayer for everyone
Who are burdened with a cross
Jesus carried His for all mankind
The world will always feel His loss.

MY JOE

Even if the storm clouds gather
Reach out I will hold your hand
We have traveled many miles
In this great and wondrous land.

A friend sent to me an angel
When we met so long ago
Seems angels guarded us in life
On gossamer wings that never show.

It's good being remembered
For you Rita I write this poem
Sometime maybe we can visit
In your new Florida home.

Joe I loved you very dearly
Caring for my every need
Being there when ere I stumbled
A kind and generous deed.

My love for you will last forever
You were the very best
So let the storm clouds gather
We'll manage to stand that test.

Our great love keeps us together
You reach out and take my hand
Darling Joe I loved you dearly
To me you were a precious man.

[MY JOE—continued]

We traveled life's great highways
Reaching out from shore to shore
You protect me from all danger
My love is yours forevermore

I made a promise
I would write for you some word
The promise will be kept
My duty will not shirk.
I'll present this poem to you
Filled with all my love and feelings
For a man so tried and true.

THOUGHT

A pound good prevention
An ounce a measure we need
A pinch of happiness to be sharing
A cup of hope to succeed.

A glass of faith not forgotten
An inch of mercy to someone sad
A peck of real emotion
A purchase to make someone glad.

Find a reason for doing or giving
Scatter clouds, chase away blues
A rainbow you can watch
A chapter of life you must not lose.

A bundle of courage for everyone
A barrel of laughs to make them shout
Take your angel along to hold you close
A reason what life is about.

We want things to fit like a glove
A prayer will be in style
The tomorrows might bring pleasure
For someone somewhere worthwhile.

RED BRICK MANSION

There is a red brick mansion
Located on route four
Enclosed by a quaint iron fence
A picturesque home of yore.

People living in this place
Are very happy because
The rolling lawn and beautiful trees
Are something worth applause.

The driveway leading up the hill
Midst flower gardens large and small
Planted and lighted night and day
Growing in stately elegance
To show a wanderer's way.

A brook flows quietly
At the foot of the hill
Just like a story book
Children playing so happy and free
As spring comes alive in cranny and nook.

May the people who live in this mansion
Have memories that reach to the sky
Enjoy life at its very best
And never have reason to cry.

LOVE

Hear the sounds of thundering hooves
Wind blowing in the trees
Bright sun shining on
Mountains and streams
Laughter wafting in the breeze.

The whistle of a moving train
As it rumbles on the way
Carrying fuel for energy
Soon will give away.

To planes soaring cross the sky
As rockets flying through space
What are they trying to prove
About men living there, why the race?

To reach the unknown, the money spent
So many staving on earth
Almighty God gave us a world
To enjoy its real worth.

He gave us life, a chance to pray
So listen, learn, understand
I'd rather the future would bring to all
Love in this wondrous land.

LIFE

This little poem
Is all about
Someone I used to know
Always taking
Never sharing
Why? I would
Like to know
Finding faith
With everyone
Seldom see them smile
Never, never trying
To help or walk
That extra mile
Well time has passed
My life keeps moving on
I hope someday someone will say
May heaven be her home.

She tried to live and forgive
To anyone is need
Living, loving, learning to grow
Just walk along a lonely path
The hours quickly go
Somewhere, sometime a better place
Our God has told us so.

BRAVE

We cannot gain great wisdom
Without willingness to learn
No way can we buy happiness
It must be ours to earn.

Walk a mile share a smile
E'en to the path is long
I must not fret or show regret
Just be brave and strong.

So with the wisdom that I gain
I'll never close the door
But look around and help someone
That is what life is for.

HE CARES

Where were you the time I ask
Answer to my prayer
I thought, was I forgotten
Yet you were always there.

So asking again God walk with me
At beginning of each day
When I falter, pick me up
Help me on my way.

2002

Live to enjoy the shining sun
Smile through a cloudy day
Her the children singing
As they go along their way.

Flower buds are bursting
Gloom is not for lovely things
Smiles bring more happiness
Harsh words only sting.

We need the rain a blessing
The warmth of days in spring
Need love for one another
To you I'm offering.

Beauty of all livings things
Full of joy and laughter
No one knows how soon
Comes the calling of the Master.

That is why I spend my days
Doing my very best
The years grow fast in number
Giving life a test.

Do what you can, make life worthwhile.
As through the day you trod
When no one seems to understand
Remember there is a God.

THE ARTIST

At a showing I enjoyed
The fifteenth of December
At the governor's mansion in Illinois
I will long remember.

An artist with his magic touch
Paint brush in his hand
Working on a masterpiece
About our glorious land.

I know a touch of love was there
With every stoke of brush
When the work was finished
A silent quiet hush.

It filled my heart to bursting
Happiness, dreams a firm desire
Wondering why people—everyone
Might aim a little higher.

I watched artists in Austria
London, York, Milan and Wales
They loved to talk, sketch and tease
While sipping foreign ales.

LITTLE FRIENDS

My little neighbors across the street
Nancy, Jake and Kee-Kee cat
Greet each day with hi-hello
Always ready for a chat

Ernie, Albert and two Lindas
Kate, Mary, Ken and Stacey
Jim Crowley had a big black dog
Also played drums like crazy.

My husband Joe liked Jake the best
Because he loved to talk
Always asking what he could do
Or would Joe like to take a walk.

The time to me most precious
Were their visits every day
Because soon they all grew up
Were out of school and moved away

Most are married now I know
Have children of their own
If ever they can visit
My house can be there second home.

WORDS

Think of a word you heard many times
Or any other you might choose
Soon realizing a poem has been written
Because you find use, free and sure in refuse.

Gold in the golden rule
A fact in satisfaction
Rule in a ruler you use in school
Act is in a fraction.

There is a vest in every harvest
A mile in every smile
Rain can be found in rainbow
A whirl in each worthwhile.

Great things may appear in laughter
Paint and action in anticipation
Also a bear and bar in break
Stop a moment for heaven's sake.

No matter where you travel
What distance the miles might be
You will find way, war, wear in weary
Also find rest in mystery.

IN MEMORY

We salute the heroes
As they the flag unfurled
Knowing many loves were lost
In this our freedom world.

The enemy thought our country known for fame
Would fall apart for sure
Anger felt, tears were shed
But we will long endure.

The landmarks in New York City
So many lives were given
In Washington and Pennsylvania
Those souls went straight to heaven.

We must remember citizens
Hang in there; hear our plea
Pray for loved ones left behind
We will have liberty

It's time to search the U.S. wide
We beg and we implore
They had no right, cause us to fight
Its time to close the door.

CARE

Never let a day go by
Without offering a prayer
For some friend or relative
Just show them you care.

I'm hoping someone sometime
Will say a prayer for me
And that people everywhere
Will live in harmony.

May God bless families we love
As through each day we trod
A quiet moment will be spent
Being thankful to our God.

It seems everyone is busy
Trying to make a living
Maybe we should stop and think
Each day is a Thanksgiving.

It matters little this I know
About what you have on your mind
Wish them well in every way
Do not be unkind, grasp their hand
It might brighten up their day.

DEER

Now I wonder as I wander
Stopping by the garden gate
Will the flowers bloom all winter
Or will Jack Frost set a date.

Oh how I enjoy the sunset
Setting slowly in the west
We could use a nice rain shower
The sun can take a rest.

Soon its time to say my prayers
Having enjoyed a glorious day
Come and visit in my garden
If you travel down my way.

The deer still come in early morn
Eating flowers and leaves as they go
They love roses, geraniums and hibiscus
Just like putting on a show.

We do not mind, they are hungry
They are part of God's creation
He created this great earth
Never show anger and vexation.

I BELIEVE

Travel the road of life slowly
Each day that passes by
Shed those tears of sadness
Wings of hope to reach on high.

Grief will cause loneliness
Creating great distress
Say a word of thoughts to cheer
Leave some pleasure show progress.

Time is a gift my friend
Twenty four hours make a day
Sixty minutes in an hour
Any second might cause delay.

A year of life seems a long time
Twelve months to make things right
Think back on the years you lived
Hold on to memories real tight.

So as the years pass quickly
Sometime tears overflow
Say a prayer the angels listen
And God lets our feelings show.

LIFE

Sometimes when I start to write
My thoughts are far away
Thinking of the yesteryears
Dreams of joy will never stray.

A family filled with love and laughter
And friends at school to know
Those days were filled with pleasure
Learning helped us all to grow.

Growing up we realize
Obligations are a must
Do not throw away the knowledge
In others you must trust.

So as the years of youth are gone
Memories, love will last
We now live in the present
Our days go by so fast.

Never think life is over
Make new friends every day
No road of life is paved with gold
Love of God will always stay.

TWENTY-O-ONE

They terrorized our homeland
Twin towers, Pentagon, loving people
Airlines suffered many losing life
Horror of it there is no equal.

A date will linger long in memory
September eleven twenty-o-one
Taking many of united people
Whose daily work had just begun.

Trying to shake our faith and freedom
With hate cause agony in our land
They thought not of crusaders
Who would search hand in hand.

Yes we will remember nine eleven 2001
Flights 95, 93 and 77 eleven
All who perished by terrorism
Their angels took them straight to heaven.

Our Master has their names engraved
In his holy book to show
Showered them with blessings
For all the world to know
About evil people harming America
The country we love so.

CELEBRATION

Don, Rita and Karen gave me a birthday party
At number Ten Foxfords Chase
All who came enjoyed themselves
Bonding friendships and adding grace.

My grandchildren add up to five
Karen, Rick, Tim, Denny, Trish
A great time when all together
As much as anyone could wish.

Great grandchildren number four
Stephanie, Chelsea, Callahan and Joe
Joe could not attend the party
He was visiting his grandfather in Ohio.

In-laws Tom, Spud, Jack, Great-great grandson Chase
Dolores, Johanna, Heather, Bill, Jennifer and Dana
Fran and Bill, Aaron, also Nancy
The conversation rang joyous, plain and fancy.

Henry came alone as Imogene was in Maine
We all missed her presence
Because my family loves to entertain.
She was missed but with us in remembrance.

Receiving many gifts, cards and a telephone call
From friends, nieces, nephews, cousins scattered in many states
Notes from Sis, and Sisters Pauletta and Frances Mary too
All so special and precious, made me feel ten feet tall

Flower bouquets, balloons, birthday cakes and candy
Messages from North, South, East and West

California, Illinois, Iowa, Florida and Texas
All received and brought much happiness.

I may be ninety years of age
But still feel so young at heart
Thanks to all who came to celebrate
And left loving memories to fill my heart.

Frances Helen Kunzweiler
July 20, 2004

MONTH AFTER MONTH

As I think about tomorrow
Traveling to a distant shore
I must stay at home, keep busy
Writing about our months to endure.

January

    There is Jay, Jury, Ray and Jan
    Which means winter has just began.

February

    Has a fury bear, year and fear
    And presidents' holidays all kids will cheer.

March

    Has car and charm, time to achieve
    Comes in like a lion, can you believe.

April

    This month has rip rap ail pail and rail
    Spring in the offing, time to exhale.

May

    Find am, ma, my and don't forget mother
    School is soon dismissed, hope you recover.

June

    Not any words, time to travel
    So fathers go sit back and unravel.

July
> There are no words to apply
> So watch fireworks and let the flags fly.

August
> Has gust tag stag sag, how quickly summer passes
> Time for school, so back to the classes.

September
> Has best, rest, temper and ember
> Things from summer you will remember.

October
> A robot Halloween dressed child
> Greeting them will give you a smile.

November
> Certain words I know you have heard
> So keep busy thinking while stuffing the bird.

December
> Find a bed, beer, reed and someone in need
> With kids hoping Santa is picking up speed.

Try each month finding a new thing
Keeping busy makes your heart sing.

SAIL AWAY

To sail away on a summer day
On a majestic ocean liner
Arriving one week later
On the island Medina.

Flowers every hue and color
We enjoyed the fragrance
Showing grateful appreciation
Bring back fond memories
Of my first Hawaii vacation.

If you sit around worrying
Wondering just what to plan
Asking others what should we do
Who really don't give a damn.

Buy things small to accommodate
A cheery empty place
Buy something that leaves memories
Take home for style and grace.

When a times comes you get lonesome
Take no pity on yourself
If a problem causes anxiety
Hide it on a forgotten shelf.

THE UNITED STATES OF AMERICA

Alabama

      I went to Alabama, a banjo on my knee.

Alaska

      Traveled to Alaska for moose and bear to see.

Arkansas

      This is called a southern state.

Arizona

      They say Arizona has an altitude that's great.

California

      Is a state when ocean meets the sky.

Colorado

      A great state to give new skis a try.

Connecticut

      I like the name of this state where you can cut a rug.

Delaware

      Wear a fancy dress and do the jitterbug.

Florida

      Another great state surrounded by the sea.

Georgia

      Here they grow pecans and peaches for you and me.

Hawaii

      I did my best to give the Hula a try.

Idaho

      Ida helped me dig potatoes with a ho and hi.

Illinois

      I made noise in the state that makes people ill.

Indiana

      Watching race drivers really was a thrill.

[THE UNITED STATES OF AMERICA—continued]

Iowa
> The corn in this state grows ten feet high.

Kansas
> Wheat harvest keeps farmers busy and tensions really fly.

Kentucky
> Has a derby where people come from many nations.

Louisiana
> Blues are famous here so join in the celebrations.

Maine
> An eastern seaboard state where lobster is a treat.

Maryland
> A visit to Maryland cannot be beat.

Massachusetts
> A state with almost the longest name.

Michigan
> They have china in this state, no I'm not insane.

Minnesota
> Play tennis with Tina, Tom, Sam and Tim

Mississippi
> A state with three double letters; spell it backward for a grin.

Missouri
> The state where I was born.

Montana
> A place where you find buffalo and big horn.

Nebraska
> Wheat is raised here, this is no joke.

Nevada
> Make the wrong bet here and soon you will be broke.

New Jersey
> This state has sea, seen, yes and sew.

New Hampshire
> People here hire those in the know.

New Mexico
> Things to see keeps you on the go.

New York
> A place to find an excellent show.

North Carolina
> People here are all really great.

North Dakota
> If you wish to visit, do not hesitate.

Ohio
> A hi and a ho makes you concentrate.

Oklahoma
> Another state where the song is really o-k-l-a great.

Oregon
> A place to rest and songs are sung.

Pennsylvania
> Where you can hear the Liberty Bell rung.

Rhode Island
> A land of enchantment, all agree.

South Carolina
> A place in the south where the wind blows free.

South Dakota
> Let's travel there for many things to see.

Tennessee
> Another state with double letters.

Texas
> A state where cowboys never ride better.

Utah
> Where we sat and had a chat.

[THE UNITED STATES OF AMERICA—continued]

Vermont

> Maple syrup here might make you fat.

Virginia

> Gin in this would make me dizzy.

Washington

> A tour of Boeing would keep me busy.

West Virginia

> The place where people are homespun great.

Wisconsin

> Wonderful cheese is found in this state.

Wyoming

> The end of the line
> A song I will sing
> And soar above
> Like a bird on the wing.

JIM

This guy I know not a mystery
I have seen him through the ages
He is a generous and gentle person
The story would fill many pages.

He lives in Springfield, Illinois
Resides five thirty-five south Glenwood
With his beloved dog "Arnie"
Let this be understood.

Arnie is a miniature Schnauzer
Indeed a man's best friend
Devoted and gentle as a giant
From morning 'til days end.

The Master's name Fitzgerald
Irish as Patty's pig
Please don't ask him ever
To do the Irish jig.

Their home is three stories tall
And each floor truly a wonder
Model trains occupy the third level
They magically run from wall to wall.

Living there for many years
Gives Jim pride and sheer delight
If any time you visit
His trains will focus your sight.

He attended Cathedral Boys' High
Along with my son Don

Now he comes to visit Florida
A place I feel where he belongs.

He grew up at five thirty five
With memories that add merit
When mom & dad went to heaven
The home place was his to inherit.

Jim when you come to visit
Bring Arnie along for the ride
He will get along with Jacques.
Our Schnauzer and our pride.

Jim died May 26, 2006
God rest his soul.

ME

Do you remember yesterday
Did your work kept you busy
Pulling weeds, washing windows
Until feeling dizzy.

Maybe what you did yesterday
Run the sweeper, mop the floor
All these things are necessary
Like shopping at the grocery store.

I also like clothes, shoes, jewelry
Eating out a real pleasure
I sit down rhyme a line
Someone someday might treasure

Tomorrow comes, yesterday was
It happens year after year
I feel angels pray for me
We never see them, they are near.

FOLLOW ME

Choirs of angels
Were singing
I listened quietly
Then someone beckoned
Come and follow me.

I was awakened suddenly
From this marvelous dream
I found the power to get busy
Regaining self esteem.

Must get busy doing things
I put off yesterday
Yet it was great dreaming
My thoughts were in disarray.

If you tried to call me
Got no answer of the phone
My thoughts were with the angels
I was not alone.

In your quiet time remember
Take a chance and borrow
Happy thoughts you've stored up
For tomorrow and tomorrow.

LORETTA

It seems only yesterday
I said goodbye to you
My fondest memories remain
Even through the times were few.

You picked me up, took me to church
Out to lunch and such
Then we would talk for hours
Those times, they meant so much.

You live on in memory
And prayers they I say
There is a happier tomorrow
Where we will meet again someday.

I know the angels came to greet you
When you reached heaven's gate
And you'll remember we who loved you
Because your life on earth was great.

TRAVEL

A smile can ease emotions
That cause one frustrations
A frown causes wrinkles
Furrowed brows last for durations

A prayer each day a good way
As you travel life's road
Never dread what lies ahead
Seek help to carry the load.

Today is what yesterday was
Yet tomorrow never comes
Remember when you eat the bread
There are birds to eat the crumbs.

So with eyes to see
And hands to touch
How can anyone say
That's not so much.

THE PANEL

A masterpiece of beauty
Hangs in hallowed place
The nature and the magic
Leaves a smile on every face.

The age of those viewing
Be they nine or ninety-two
Everyone enjoys the pleasure
Seeing visions pass in review.

Brought to life by brilliant art man
Watching people stop and stare
Reliving youth in every minute
Without a worry or care.

Enjoy the masterpiece dear Marvin
Bring a smile to Anita's face
She will know what you are thinking
She emanated style and grace.

Sit quietly for a moment
Think of life in ages past
Let the inspiration guide you
Having memories sure to last.

Joe Burlini was the master
For this work of art so grand
About his feelings for Anita
What a kind and generous man.

We offer special prayers and thanks
For Joe and Sue, and Marvin A.

It's like standing in the wings
Of life in an unforgettable way.

Paying tribute in remembrance
For a lady regal and grand
Now the angels ever watchful
Strolling with her hand in hand.

LADDER

A thought just came to me
Someone might need a ladder
To reach eternity
Then everyone could climb
A rung each day of their life
An adventure of feeling free.

If finding that was slow
A longer stride you could try
Might get you closer
To where planes and astronauts fly.

Look down with amazement
View life below in its glory
A vision of what God created
Oceans, deserts, rivers, forests
Believe in creation a mysterious story..

My dreams cost me nothing
Still I often wonder
If the farther up we climb
Would the noise be louder
When it storms and starts to thunder.

LOUISE, FRIEDA AND ME

Have you ever visited any farm
That sows all kinds of seed
To plant their fields for many
Who have animals and poultry to feed.

We had a small farm
Many years ago
Raised all kinds of veggies
To fill our lauder to overflow.

We would not grow hungry
When winter months were bare
No lights or power of any kind
The dark cellar was filled with care.

Always early in the Fall
Which usually was September
My mom filled three hundred jars
Of beans, corn, peas, all cold pack
And more jams than I remember.

I never liked to milk the cow
My sister Louise did that
Who sat beside her patiently
She would squirt some at the cat.

I liked cooking, doing dishes
That was my daily chore
Except when it was thrashing time
Sometime feeding forty or more.

My sister Frieda the oldest
Always busy as a bee

She liked being noticed
For all young men to see.

These days still live in memory
When the harvest turned out great
All farmers families gathered
It was time to celebrate.

Now everything comes frozen
In cans, bottles and sealed plastic
Young folks today will never know
Life back then was fantastic.

STORMS

If tears could tell a story
Mine would be for safety
From all the hurricanes fury
Why everyone must hurry.

When they inform us to leave
Take all important things
When all you own is precious
With thought of joy they bring

So up to Macon, Georgia
Three hundred plus miles away
Many folks ran out of petrol
The reason traffic delay.

A trip of about six hours
Making time important to most
A million cars, trucks carrying cargo
Were traveling coast to coast.

Wind caused much damage
Hit the area eighty or more
Roofs off, water poring in
Every inch of furniture and floor

Difficult for families to endure
Losing keepsakes and remembrances
May angels keep watch over all
Add prayer for better chances.

We wonder why this happens
Charley, Frances, Jeanne in a row

Was the earth surrounded with humanity
That caused oceans to overflow..

DO YOU SUPPOSE

When I knock on the pearly gate
Hoping no one will say
You're not good enough to enter
I heard you did not pray.

Then comes another question
I thought you made a motion
To ignore your enemies
What a foolish notion.

Why must there be such feelings
About our fellow men
Since the day of our creation
The world has been full of sin.

As each one looks into his heart
Saying I have nothing to tell
Maybe the gate of heaven will close
We all might go to hell?

LEARNING

Sitting down to write a poem
Someone might enjoy
Or bring a gift to treasure
By a little girl or boy.

A book to read for knowledge
Take them back in time
See a smile come to their face
To ease a lonely mind.

We must show them pleasures
Give a chance to live and learn
Not causing pain for anyone
Should be of great concern.

A prayer by we who care
Will give no cause for grief.
A mile is found in every smile
All anger would be brief.

Never let anyone put you down
As if you were a clod
Remember each and everyone
Has an angel sent by God.

TRYING

Trying very willingly
To lend a helping hand
It will give us pleasure
Lead us to understand.

Living can be beautiful
A pathway easy we trod
By caring, loving, sharing
All with the help of God.

When we let despair and loneliness
Follow wherever we go
The road to peaceful living
Will never be easy, I know.

Remember others have heartaches
A road you don't travel alone
Still finding the way to happiness
By good deeds they have sown.

UPSIDE DOWN

Smile, laugh, love, frown
The first makes friends, second bring joy
Third fills the world and it abounds.
Fourth clouds the face with ugliness and
Turns your whole life upside down.

THOUGHTFUL

Enjoy the days of happiness
Our tender years are few
Seek all life's little pleasures
That present themselves to you.

Our road to love, peace and joy
May be found in each small step
And loneliness will quickly pass
Being a friend to all you've met.

Best of all good things for everyone
I'll reach out a helping hand
In need to share their burdens
With love in this wondrous land.

Be of help, show understanding
Maybe solve a problem or two
Give them hope for the future
A small thing to do.

THANKS

To write a poem short and sweet
A thought or two I might repeat
Perhaps a chance might come your way
Catch that gold ring, do not delay.

Take a walk, climb a hill
Watching children, what a thrill
Listen to bluebird's song
Will make you happy all day long.

Wander by a babbling brook
Rhyme a line, read a book
Then when the day is done why fret
You have not made a million yet.

Keep trying and remembering
When winter's gone then comes spring
The wind, the sky, the sun all free
Bring happy thoughts to you and me.

We can wish upon a star
Traveling highways near and far
Why worry if you have no wealth
Then God you can enjoy good health.

LEADER

I saw you sitting all alone
Beside a quiet brook
A day in summer beautiful
Not even branches shook.

My thoughts were filled with things unreal
Like peace on earth for all
Say a prayer, God listens
Soon the night will fall.

Please do not waste a moment
Just think of how and when
All mankind lives in harmony
As when the world began.

Throughout the place we call earth
May we take time to pray
Let us show what peace is worth
Have faith, God leads the way.

PEACE

Walk along a lonely road
Find peace in each step
Pause with thoughts in silence
About the Lord when he wept.

EDUCATION

Every prayer is answered
For happiness each day
Foolish thoughts and idle moments
Oft times get in the way.

So dear Lord I am asking
Hear each person's humble call
Because we all need help
Knowing you love us all.

Ashland in Cass County Illinois
Not known for fame or people grand
Respect was known for everyone
A good education was the plan.

Attended Yatesville grade school
All eight grades in one big room
Everyone studied diligently, no talking out loud
To make parents and teacher proud.

Don't pity us for what we learned
As each class and grade did their share
And the knowledge was the greatest
Few schools today can compare.

Yatesville school still stands today
Run down and quite forlorn
It educated many students
Who were all American born.

MAN

When you really feel important
And your ego is in full bloom
Are you taking life for granted
You're the wisest in the room?

You feel you are brilliant
Would leave a great big hole
Follow those instructions
They will humble any soul.

Take a bucket full of water
Put your hand in to the wrist
Pull it out the hole remaining
Is how little you will be missed.

Fill the bathtub with lots of water
Stir about and splash galore
Then stop in just a minute
Its calm as was before.

The moral of the story
Do the best you can
Be proud but please remember
There is no indispensable man.

HILL 875

TO NORVAL

Strange places we read about
Da Nang, Cam Ranh, Qui Nhon
Like pieces of a puzzle
Continuous marathon
American forces everywhere
Keeping right in stride
Spirit the greatest ever
Deep feelings they have inside.

Being far from home not forgetting
Their thoughts, how to survive
Though losses were suffered, bravery shown
When they took Hill 875

Based at Tuy Hoa, men in green and blue
With help from Bien Hoa you see
While Can Tho a fortress river patrol
Soon may these names be history.

Men on the ground important
At Cu Chi, Di An, Song Be
Nha Trang, Chu Lai, Pleiku
Our courageous infantry
They will win battles, won't forget
Our armed forces the greatest alive
A promise they made their buddies
Not returning from Hlll 875.

FREEDOM

If you do not like our country
Go back from where you came
We will pledge our allegiance
Just like a burning flame.

On national holidays we celebrate
With bands marching on our streets
Proudly presenting our colors
If you don't like it, please retreat.

This is America, we sing its praises
And by faith walk hand in hand
A great nation known for freedom
Whose culture long will stand.

Being proud we stand for liberty
We like our Uncle Sam
They came to blast our buildings
A wakeup call for us to keep our country grand.

Rid our shores of terrorists
With man, planes and ships at sea.
Search out enemies from everywhere
Long we pray to be free.

We will have freedom in America
Many years to celebrate
Let our people live in peace and quiet
We love our country, it's first rate.

HELLO

The prayers I've said
Silently and alone
Helped ease the pain
Like an old refrain
And suddenly the sun shone
On a brighter day
With thoughts that stray
To the time we had together
So we must leave
And show concern
In all kinds of weather.

Many times we find
Life passes us by
We must wake and realize
The burden might be heavy
So wipe away
The tears that fall
Tomorrow ever comes
Reach out have good thoughts
About one you love
Find out your hand is
Not all thumbs.

FAMILY

There were ten in our family
We were a happy bunch
Living only a few yards from school
We could go home for lunch.

Our job was to work in the garden
Pick beans and shell the peas
And when not done properly
Our mom it did not please.

Frieda was the oldest then came along Louise
Frances was the next in line
The older would always tease.

Next came Charles Jr.
Followed by mischievous Tom
In a short time then Norval
Golly gee, hardly a year was gone.

Russell showed up in a couple of years
Followed by Bobby Gene
We all thought that was enough
The walls were bursting at the seam.

We were a happy family
Never having many toys
A tricycle, bicycle and red wagon
Were shared by all five boys.

We would go to town on Saturday night
Ashland, Illinois was sits name

A place to spend our ten cent piece
Those memories will long remain.

Today young folks have everything
Scooters, roller blades, bikes, cars that zing
I often wonder when their future holds
Will they have memories that mean anything.

I wish them all the very best
Happy years to feel carefree
What lies ahead, a mystery
In this great land of liberty.

FIRST COUSINS

Frieda and Carl started with Ruth Ann
Then Helen Lea by name
Eddie was the lad and third in line
The last, Carolyn, also known as Jane.

Louise and Ray began with Jerry
Shirley Jean soon came along
Linda Sue their next in line
Always singing a happy song.

Frances and Joe had Donald Joseph
Named for his wonderful dad
Three years later came Rheta Louise
The greatest treasure we had.

Charles and Doris had Patricia and Karen
Two blondes with lots of vim
Both were petite and small
Their dad was tall and slim.

Tom and Dolores issued Rich
In a couple years came Jim
Always pleasure to be around
With a howdy and big grin.

Norval and Mary came up with three
Maureen, Tom and Terry
Three of a kind with lots on their mind
But Terry sometimes contrary.

Russell and Dorothy delivered four
Kathleen, Barbara, Gregory and Don

They were all very different
Like a wonderful marathon.

Bob, the youngest had no family
He liked to move around
Living in Las Vegas for many years
We were lucky when he could be found.

This is the end of first cousins
Many of the family now laid to rest
Those remaining need to keep memories
And strive to do their very best.

DREAM

If today I have a dream
Wishing it come true
It would be love around the world
And skies forever blue.

My wish for peace and quiet time
Help for all in need
Blessed with health and happiness
Then I might plant a seed.

Of joy, days filled with laughter
Along the right of way
Hoping now and ever after
All believe, take time to pray.

For each and every dream we have
Will guide us through the night
Awaken us, so we may see
Peace for all, no cause for fright.

May my dream come true sometime
I'll be ready, willing to share
The best life has to offer
Showing each I really care.

OUR ANGEL

We each have an angel
Given to us we know
By God who is master
Traveling with us where we go.

Many times we oft forget
Thinking no one really cares
When sorrow creeps into our hearts
Angels stand by with repairs.

Do not feel lost or lonely
When you miss a lifetime friend
Find someone to care for
Your sorrow will soon end.

Life is good for each and everyone
Even when we face a test
We're all for one and one for all
Our angel knows what's best.

Guardian Angel stay with me
Especially if I stray
I'll walk the path you travel
With you leading the way.

MY VISIT

The buildings on West Washington and Monroe
Staffed with beautiful people rare
A tower of education
In these times of trial and error

I like going to visit
With some friends who now reside
Within this place of beauty
Where love, faith and prayer abide

They have a student body
Girls from throughout our land
If anyone has problems
They're given a helping hand.

Being taught basic studies
Affairs of church and state
When anniversaries roll around
They pause to celebrate.

They send teachers to many cities
Helping educate the youth
Building for God and freedom
Guided by the hand of truth.

Sisters Innocent, William and Benedict
With Pauletta are the ones I know best
Retired from rigorous duties
They earned and deserve the rest.

Talented nuns and students
Produced a recording with care

To celebrate Christ's coming
Magnificent savior-fare.

The stately group of buildings
Enhanced by Dominican nuns
Places to worship and relax
When day's work is done.

May God bless them one and all
Though humble my wish be
Faith and love guiding from above
What a lasting memory.

My thanks for the privilege
Being able to know, visit and see
That faith is the answer to happiness
Loving kindness the key.

DAY OF HOPE

A smile showing you care so important
A child visiting a dream world
Being carried away to an enchanted forest
Expecting, anticipating a beautiful future
With someone you're longing to see.

Giving your talents to create a world
Make believe, bring a ray of hope
Saying a prayer could mean the difference
Between happiness and complete failure.
Let not a day pass unless
You've tried to lift
The burden of one less fortunate.
Because God willing their cross like His
Could have been too heavy to carry.
May the pathway be strewn with rose petals
For each and multiplied a million times.

THE FARM 1937

Come to visit once in awhile
Leave your troubles home
Let's talk about the good times
As around the farm we roam.

The countryside of God's creation
With meadows where wildflowers grow
A crystal brook we waded in
Was many ages ago.

I like remembering good times
Wonderful days of youth
Tiny one room schoolhouse
We were taught, tell the truth.

We reminisce in wonder
About the beautiful people we knew
My feelings go out to the young folks
Their memories will be few.

You gave me love to make me smile
Never failed to walk that mile
I return to you a gift of mine
Wishing everyday your sun will shine.

YOUR HAND

Someone you know might need your help
You could extend your hand
Offer a friendly greeting
If lonesome, time you might spend.

Many days pass in each one's life
All have idle time
My wish to enjoy the future
May I always to others be kind.

Stretch out your hand, make somebody feel
A friend they found so true
When resting your weary head at night
There's a God to watch over you.

A.M.

Morning came shining sun on blades of green grass
Dew drops made them glisten like an hour glass
My good intentions pulling weeds
From lawn and by the fence
Hands willing to get started
My mind a little dense.

Around me there was silence
Then my conscience seemed to say
I believe this morning you failed
Taking time to pray.
Very careless of me Lord
In fact, almost absurd
When occupied stay at my side
Please hear each humble word.

Keeping busy helps in life
Makes lonely hours fly
Even as I stop to gaze
At clouds drifting by
We humans dream foolishly
A rare privilege you see
Because god who created man
Gave us this liberty.

IF

A question asked, answer given
Use the knowledge for al its worth
You need not be disappointed
As you travel 'round the earth.

THINKING

Having traveled many miles
On highways cross this land
People and their friendly smiles
Is what makes living grand.

The southern states so green and lush
Pine trees proud and tall
Ocean weaves and pounding surf
With greetings, Hi you-all!

Having been to Switzerland, Germany,
Czechoslovakia, Austria and Hungary
Yugoslavia and Italy too
The beautiful city Vienna
Also Venice, really dreams come true.

All should travel to foreign lands
Seeing culture, gaining knowledge of yore
Return giving thanks for America
The greatest forevermore.

RITA

My daughter married young
Many tears were shed
Many times from happiness
Fears were felt, but love abounds
Problems surface in all families
Things to be remembered
Consideration, kindness, joy
Youth passes quickly
Pain soon forgotten
Growing older the years pass more quickly
Grandchildren soon becoming teenagers
With their own ideas, realizing this
Knowing they must go their way
Goodness never hurts, only unkindness
When you believe it shows in a smile
May I always be understanding
Wishing the best life has to offer
Only by the grace of God and with his help
Do we reach the heights of knowing
Every day of living is
More beautiful than yesterday
We can reap a harvest of love
For each tomorrow
Tomorrow becomes today.
For all her love and caring
Rita, I have no regrets
This humble prayer I am saying
Thank you for all your sharing.

AFTER THE STORM

Thunder and lightning started
Then rain came pouring down
Washed away the dirt of winter
Soon spring would abound.

Tulips, crocus and daffodils
Pushing up their heads
Blossoms greet the Easter season
Christ has risen from the dead.

Sunny summer is upon us
What more can humans ask
Hearing children at their pleasure
They grow up so fast.

They must try to conquer problems
Of the turmoil that is known
Besieging all the people
Not an individual alone.

The storm that brought us lightning
The heavy thunders roar
Gone just like the Easter season
Soon it will be July four

A different kind of celebration
That is known as Independence
When all of our nation gathers
In joyful remembrance.

HOME

Climb a mountain, swim a river
Roam throughout the land
Watching, waiting, searching
Do my best to understand,.

Travel highways, fly the skyways
Amtrak trains wherever they go
Return home tired and weary
Doing things that I love so.

Looking forward to where I'm going
Remembering places I have been
In my travels helping someone
Just to ease a little pain.

Could I help in any small way
Seeing happiness unfold
It would bring more pleasure
Than treasure of silver and gold.

Sure we each have disappointments
Even miss comforts of life
Loving and caring important
Wishing we might end the strife.

May I wish that all good things
In the future come your way
Then I'll stay at home be thankful
Spending more time to pray.

THE WIND

A flag hangs limp without the wind
Its like a day without an end
If not for prayer in time of strife
Would be like living without life.

TINY LIGHT

Light a tiny candle
Show a trace of love
Christ the savior gave us life
And watches from above.

Faith we need to guide our steps
Strength to bear the pain
Hope for everlasting knowledge
Peace on earth to gain.

WHY TRY

Why try to reach the highest peak
Life is sweeter when people speak
When seeking earthly fame recall
Faith, hope and love can conquer all.

A GARDEN RENEWED

The rains came and flowers grew
Adding a wealth of beauty
To an almost forgotten garden
That had once been attended
By loving hands, but God knows
And is understanding.

IF

If saying hello makes one happy
Think of praying for them will accomplish.

NO CLOUDS

The bells in the chapel ring out loud and clear
For someone I love may he always be near
His arms so tender his smile just right
Makes me thankful and happy each night.

Dawn of a new day no clouds in the sky
Soon the sun will appear
Causing dew drops to play hide and seek
So quickly one cannot hear
We talk of tomorrow what will it bring
Answers to dreams about love
Quietly the shadows of night will creep
As the moon shines brightly above.

SMALL SPACE

Something that grows in a garden
Can also be found on a hill
A gift for all, even strangers
Known to each as God's will.

Reach out when there are problems
Don't waste another day
Ask for help, you will find it
Nothing can stand in your way.

Life, love, laughter, happiness
May be found in a very small space
Pick a few petals for living
From a bouquet of His grace.

Never turn from forgiveness
Through pain, wear a smile on your face
Come on mankind remember
We are known as the human race.

So what if our colors are different
Life's ambition we all hope to fill
Stand straight and tall as the willow
Drink from the fountain good will.

Faith is a stranger to many
Hope a promise to all
May each be blessed with knowledge
Might reap a harvest for all.

LOVE

The happiness you shared today
I shall pass along tomorrow.

VIOLETS OF VELVET

May I pin a bouquet on my girl
Ask blessings, guard her day and night
Wishes to last forever
Violets of velvet, ribbon of white.

When I awaken each morning
A prayer keep her safe, let all see
She is always doing for others
And my Mom, she will always be.

Many times through the years
She had reason for tears
Violets of velvet I could see
Appearing to guide her everywhere.

Long live that memory
Precious the violet with ribbon of white
A small bouquet given you see
To my Mom, the dearest one
Sent to her with love from me.

THINKING

Sitting alone in the evening
Cares of the day are past
Wishing joy for everyone
Wanting happiness to last.

Like romantic lovers holding hands
Watching children at play
All these things contentment brings
Now I can put my problems away.

TIMMY

Little Timmy is only two years old
And wise as he can be
His roughish smile will win your heart
Continuously read to tease.

It's, "Grandma, I better have new shoes,
Can I go home with you;
What's Don doing, is he at work"
Which answer should I choose.

"Hey, can me and Rick stay all night
if we change our clothes
When is grandpa coming home
And watch me wiggle my toes."

Just never say, Timmy stay at home
His face gets like a storm cloud
I do not mean to brag or boast
Still couldn't be more proud.

All grown up now and moved away
Doing his own thing
But the memories being happiness
And make the angels sing.

CAREFUL

Go do things you planned
By careful on the way
Come back because I love you
More and more everyday.

POLO

There is a lonely feeling
When sitting my myself
With things I should be doing
Like dusting off a shelf.

Many hours I can spend
In the quiet of my home
Peacefulness is everywhere
While being all alone.

The crazy pace some folks keep
They're always in a whirl
To me it's much better
To relax, enjoy the world.

Well, not really all alone.
Our beloved Schnauzer is here
Of course he cannot talk to me
But adds a lot of cheer.

So lonesomeness go bother
Some who is not busy
The many things that I must do
Almost makes me dizzy.

When you have a moment
Come by and I will share
A little work to keep you busy
Maybe something to repair.

FOLLOW THE SUN

When autumn arrives in the northland
I ask you join in the fun
Of being a wandering gypsy
Come on and follow the sun,

We will drive to the southland
Then through the golden west
Pack a bag let not your feet drag
Let's search till we find the best.

Follow the sun to the deserts
Walk in sand along the seashore
Like the gold at the end of a rainbow
A dream but contentment for sure,

We can visit the land of the hula
Learn to ride waves in the surf
We're given each day to laugh
With blessings from good mother earth.

We follow the sun, let our blues run.
Sharing another beautiful day
Like the wandering gypsies told me
Loving life in a wonderful way.

A NO-NO

Never be selfish this we must learn
Do for others show concern
Give of yourself in some small way
Help then have a brighter day.

AMEN

I thank God for many blessings
From the beginning to days end
Trying to spread a little gladness
When I say each prayer amen.

COULD BE

Could be you complain too much
If true let me know today
I will be more understanding
And not turn and walk away.

Yesterday's youth will be
The backbone of tomorrow's business
And the futures hope for lasting
Peace throughout the world.

FRIDAY

It's Friday and my day to take a little 'stroll
Don't think I'll be bothered
Haven't told a soul,

Just put on my old walking shoes
Wander by myself
There are blue skies, work-days on the shelf.

Hello Friday my day,
A new friend I might seek
Just roam around like a happy clown
'til Monday of next week.

DID YOU KNOW

That God planted the seed oh happiness
In the smile of every child.

GOLDEN DAY

Good morning to a golden day
The earth wakens to the sound
Where chirping birds and happiness
Are ever to be found.

Say goodbye to loneliness
Speak hello to all
This greeting with a friendly smile
Makes me feel ten feet tall.

PRA ISE HIM

Praise him praise him Lord of creation
Showering blessings en each congregation
Help, teach us no more to sin
Kneeling in adoration we whisper Amen.

Look up in compassion see the hest
Raised to Father, Son and Holy Ghost
As the Chalice is raised on high
May we be worthy is our cry,

Guide, lead us our life through
Forgiving the sins we confessed to you
Knowing the Master will ease pain
Angels whisper the glorious refrain.

IT HAPPENED

When I pushed away the sadness
There was a ray of light
Filled with hope for each tomorrow
Put an end to all my fright.

WEEK DAYS

Days of the week keep me busy
With things around the house
Seems alone the phone does not ring
Its quiet as a little brown mouse.

Looking outside I see Tigger the cat
Creeping so slowly along
He better not catch the Cardinal
That whistles all day long.

Monday comes so does the laundry
Tuesday the ironing is a chore
Wednesday I might go shopping
Thursday a trip to the grocery store,
Friday a good day to sweep or dust
Saturday evening in church I am found
Sunday my day being lazy or goofing around.

Then time to start allover again
Something different each day
Being busy a habit of mine
Still finding time t o pray,

Where would we be without any faith
To help us when we feel pain
So when those days of the week roll around
I'm happy to start over again.

COMPLAINING

It will never be my luck
To compose a big hit song
Although the words come easy
On paper may look all wrong.

No millionaire I desire to be
Don't have the Midas touch
Just plain ole me complaining
With excuses for a crutch.

I like to walk the country road
Have thoughts of yesteryear
The old school house with scarred black boards
Hold memories ever dear,

We all learned the ABC's
Crammed in one large room
Reading, writing, arithmetic
Not how to reach the moon.

To understand young folks today
Seems a greater task
They call this the jet set age
Life for them moves too fast,

Youth are great though pleasure bent
Still we need their ideas
To conquer space live on the moon
While I enjoy golden years.

MY LOAD

Praying each day a good way
Traveling along life's road
No need to dread what is ahead
God helps me carry my load.

ACROSS THE LAND

In a distance I can hear
The freight trains rolling by
Across the fields and meadows
Their lonesome whistles cry,

They carry tractors cars and trucks
Many tons of coal
That run our mighty factories
So man might reach his goal.

I've counted freight cars many times
One hundred thirty or more
They traverse our many states
To reach each great costal shore.

The engineer a mighty man
Will do his best we know
Delivering his tons of goods
For people on the go,

I like hearing the whistles blow
From trains traveling far and wide
For this is known as freedom land
Our United states, our pride.

I BELIEVE

Complaining is a disease it warps the mind
With agony and displeasure,
By offering hope for suffering ones
Faith in God will bring a treasure.

FLING

We cross this land in private quest
Look for things that life holds best
So let everyone have their fling
Not forgetting to hear freedoms ring.

Landing of the man on Moon
This has been conquered, just how soon
Will they attempt getting to Mars
Or reach the sun and then the stars.

Who dares to say the sky is not blue
The earth not round, no one I know
Could make me ever stray
I live to accomplish many things
And learn more every day.

We have the right to offer prayer
Each in our own way
No matter what the reason
Keep faith inside every day.

LONELINESS

Loneliness don't follow me around
The reason, I won't let it
Finding you to love me
Leaves no reason to regret it,

I promise with this heart of mine
Seeing your sun will ever shine
When day ends you cease to roam
There is love surrounding you at home.

COLLINS, ARMSTROING, ALDIN — JULY 20, 1969

Hats off to Collins, man of the hour
On the far side of the moon
Maintaining power
Standing by not knowing how soon

He was *to* pick up the men from the moon,
Soaring in orbit he was alone
Communicating *to* earth that he called home

Millions were watching like you and me
To see them land near Tranquility
Armstrong, Aldin, Collins shot into space
Aboard Apollo Eleven, smiles on their face

Families were watching same as we
On July twenty sixty nine, they made history,
We feel God watched them walk on the moon
Scooping up specimen with a long handled spoon

And when they were soaring so far in space
The Angels were watching. guarding with grace.

LISTEN

A friendly hand is extended
Someone is willing *to* share
Listen and hear the heartbeat
Let them know you care,

Hands need not glisten with diamonds
To comfort someone in pain
A work worn hand filled with tenderness
Leaves memories that long remain.

RAY OF SUNSHINE

First a bud then a flower
Opens petals wide, why not
Pick it for a shut-in
Give to them with pride,

It will bring a ray of sunshine
A smile to someone's face
While there share a little laughter
It will linger with God's grace.

FEELING FUNNY

Seldom do we realize
Traveling along life's way
We're not alone, there is someone
Lonely and sad today.

So perhaps when feeling blue
You shed a little tear
Then comes that funny feeling
You find a friend is near.

Yes foolish thoughts we all have
About what some people say
It's then we must figure out
Why they don't see things our way.

May I be the first to say
Thanks and never criticize
Hoping that where I travel
I'll always find blue skies.

RICKY JOE

With sheer delight I shall write
About a little boy I know
Little yes with big ideas
We call him Ricky Joe,

A smile so like an angel
Fat cheeks and eyes that glow
Into everything at once
This rambling tyke I know.

Trying to keep up with him
Is really quite a chore
Upstairs, downstairs under chairs
Will there be much more,

Pots and pans cupboard doors
Banging to and fro
This little one a treasure
Is just fifteen months old.

With big blue eyes light brown hair
His chubby fingers twine
Around your heart with love to start
An endless page of time.

His mom and dad and sister Karen
Are away on vacation
What we are learning from this child
Is quite an education,

Prayers and love go with this poem
The reason all should know
Our pride is really showing
For our grandson Ricky Joe.

MERRY GO ROUND

Wandering in dreams to somewhere
Flying on gossamer wings
Climbing the peak of happiness
Imagination pulling the strings,

I felt the power of temptation
To swim the ocean wide
Then soared to heights of elation
On space ships where astronauts ride.

Crossing o'er mountains and deserts
Down in valleys near streams
But to catch the brass ring on the merry go round
Would be one of my favorite things.

Fantastic fascination I cherish
Wishing and dreaming are free
These things will never perish
Because they all seem real to me.

FUN

Come take a trip you won't regret
Spend a holiday interestingly
We can soar high across the sky
Or walk along the sea,

A quiet ride to greet some friends
Truly a great pleasure
The royal treatment we received
Leaves memories to treasure.

It does not take a lot of time
So relax and have some fun
We should enjoy each day living
As though life had just begun.

LOVE YOU

You came to call I wanted
To hold you in my arms
Would you have been embarrassed
Seems you have many charms,

Its not easy for me to say
The way I feel inside
For me there is no other
Will you walk by my side.
Believe I love you very much
Am I wishing on a star
Many times you seem unhappy
As though you traveled far.

Never want to make you sad
But really think you're lonely
Come see me Joe then I'll say
Please be my one and only.

END OF DAY

Twilight comes at end of day
Shrouds us in darkness soon
Fireplace logs burn brightly
Warmth fills the cool room,

Never feel the world is yours alone
Be willing to share
A smile can lighten the burden
Of someone feeling despair.

A child will laugh when happy
Joy seems to gladden each heart
Why wear a frown, lest somebody say
Did you give try a start.

As night settles down remember
Make tomorrow more pleasant, be proud
Greet someone with everything good
You will stand out from the crowd.

I KNEEL ALONE

Lord once more forgive my sins
As I kneel here
By doing evil I have hurt you
Let my ignorance disappear.

Having faith but need your strength
As through each day I trod
May I dedicate some time
And live this day for God.

HE KNOWS

The rains came and flowers grew
Adding a wealth of beauty to an
Almost forgotten garden that had
Once been attended by loving hands
But He knows and is understanding.

SEASONS

You have the heart of an angel
Asking .may I call and say to you
Darling I'm very lonely
Could you be feeling blue.
It's not easy living alone
All my evenings are free
You knew how very much
I wanted your company.

Whether the cold of winter
Spring when robins sing
Beauty of summer on the way
Time to catch the golden ring.

Autumn does not end. Enchantment
When you are close to say
Our love will be everlasting
Beside you ever I'll stay,

Winter, spring, summer, or fall
Like diadems in a crown
Greeting each like a new start in life
You never have reason to frown.

LITTLE PROBLEMS

Like the flowers in my garden
As they root and start to grow
Are the memories that still linger
Looking back on years ago.

Speak more gently, smile more often
Being good to old and young
If the golden rule is practiced
Friends are gained and fame far flung.

When a flower blooms, go pick it
Give it to a treasured one
The fragrance of the blossom
Will linger though the colors gone.

Great joy is helping others
Bringing love a hundred fold
Prayerful living brings contentment
Little problems melt like gold.

NOT BE

Live without learning
Is next to impossible
Life without praying
Will not be profitable.

LITTLE POEM

Lord I dedicate to you
A simple little poem
Give me strength and love to care
As through life I roam.

HOMEWARD BOUND WHEELS

Travel on a city street or any thoroughfare
Stop and think a moment just how did you get there
Limousine, motorcar, tractor, bus or train,
To take you there and bring you back again.

Wheels on trolley cars, airplanes, wheels on elevators
Wheels in clocks and watches, wheels on ocean freighters
Wheels to reap a harvest, wheels to mine the coal
Wheels for rovers on the moon
So man might reach his goal.

Wheels are so essential
Everyday of life
Whether a child pulling a toy
Or someone fighting for life.

Something we cannot live without
Especially folks down on the farm
After a visit they are magic to me
When I am homeward bound.

I BELIEVE

Harvesting a bouquet of happiness is hopeless without friends.

A MIGHTY HAND

We had so many rains this spring
Floods washed away the land
There are some who don't believe
God rules with a mighty hand

Folks complain about high prices
When they should wear a grin
Complaining gets us no place
We should all begin.

Giving thanks for everyday
Our country stands with pride
So live today and shout hooray
Freedom is on our side.

JOY

One cup of love
One half cup of cheerfulness
Three cups of faith
A pound of forgiveness,

A barrel of friendship
One pinch of pride
A bushel of gratitude
With prayer on the side.

Mix, stir until blended
Add a million intentions
Spread a ton of joy
In proper dimensions.

CALICO CARPET 1995

The world is a calico carpet
The master made with love and care
Divided into many countries
Wishing all were willing to share.

Red for the blood on the battlefield
White snow on mountains high
Green in the valleys and forests
Blue for his heavenly sky.

People live on this calico carpet
I wonder why all can't agree
To seek gold at the end of the rainbow
Watch a silver sun set on the sea.

Pause at a stream as it rushes by
See trees swaying high above
Each moment to me is precious
In this calico world that I love.

Yes He made this calico carpet
The creation one of his best
The sun rises for him each morning
A yellow moon shines on request,

Calico carpet, homes filled with love
We are each hoping I know
To enjoy peace on this land He created
After all, it is his home show.

LITTLE PINK ROSE

You search for it in a garden
Among hilly ranges everywhere
Looking to see if you might find it
With other flowers growing there,

Petals soft as velvet
Center like spun told
Leaves of waxen beauty
Thorny stems you cannot hold.

The fragrance that it carries
Tells not where it grows
Given to me by a lover
A beautiful little pink rose.

I've looked in shops selling blossoms
Of everything that grows
Asking if they knew the origin
Of this tiny delicate rose.

,In memory it will live forever
I guess heaven only knows
Because my loved one said He created
For me this precious little pink rose.

HIS CHILDREN

The world is filled with God's children
Suffering from hunger, pain and riot
With one life to live we must learn to give
Until our voices are quiet.

JOYS

The sun casts a shadow when shining
There' a glow when the full moon beams
A train whistles at the crossing
Rivers are fed from small streams.

It' a joy to see our flag flying
The banner of red, white and blue
Like the promise of life everlasting
My love for you is true.

Golden grain before a harvest
Green of grass in the spring
The peace and quiet abounding
Cardinals and Whippoorwills sing.

These things may be enjoyed by everyone
Who loves their neighbors and friends
Laughter the key for a dreamer like me
For there is no money to spend.

LOVE

Darling let me love you
Each hour of everyday
Not wanting to be selfish
No matter what you say,

Did you hear me whisper
When we were alone
Today the sun shone brighter
Because you are my own.

BETTER THIS WAY

No one is forced to get on their knees
Nor are they commanded to pray
But I know it lightens burdens
Journeying on my way.

I will help when you have problems
Perhaps can ease the pain
Brush the tear from a tiny tot
So they might play again.

Run an errand if needed
Visit a shut-in or two
Write a note to a loved one
Which is long over due.

Really not forced to do these things
Never a demand that I pray
Yet doing a deed for someone in need
Will make living better every day.

A POET ME

A poet me well yes why not
There's time to look and learn
Think about people, love and life
Seems there's never ending strife
But a poet me this much I know
God's love and faith might make it go.

MY LOVE

My iridescent love like a bubble
Sparkles like diamonds you see
A heart filled with yearning
For your returning, keep me company.

Clear as a pool of water
Bright like the sun on high
Smooth as the feel of velvet
Soft as the butterfly

Wild the surf from the ocean
Cool the breath of spring.
Silent a lover's whisper
Quiet the ripple of a stream.

My iridescent love is beautiful
Pure as the fallen snow
Tell the heavenly angels
They let the whole world know.

HIS CARE

Stillness of the earth at night
When covered o'er with snow so white
Like a sentinel is waiting
Glad to see the morning light.

As he goes home from his duties
Stops in church to say a prayer
Asking God when night comes again
Please keep me in your care.

JOY FROM THE YOUNG

The little rabbit hops around
Upon the snowy frozen ground
Stops to look this way and that
He knows my neighbor has a cat.

I know that Spring will finally come
The snow will melt with warming sun
Streams and rivers will run full
Then grass to mow and weeds to pull.

I like the seasons one and all
But summer brings most pleasure
The kids around my swimming pool
Enjoying life to fullest measure
They keep me young, have tales to tell
Sometimes quite a bunch
Just to celebrate we have a picnic lunch.

Years soon pass that is why
We must enjoy each season
Why argue what the powers seem
There is no rhyme or reason
It's my aim not to complain
How foolish could I be
Not to look up and see the love
Surrounding you and me.

LITTLE TRICIA

I must not scold or fuss about
Being nine I must not shout
Just help with dishes, beds and such
When I want to play so much.

With four more in the family now
Things I do will help somehow
But when a movie is on TV
That's when mom starts calling me.

See what Rick wants; help Timmy some
Get some shoes for Denny
For every time I have to run
Wish I would get a penny.

Wondering was it all worthwhile
Help cook, clean, do the dishes
I guess it really was because
Mom brought home baby Tricia.

LOOK

Look for the road to happiness
Try, it's easy to find
Loving, caring, doing, sharing
Gives one peace of mind.

CAPTURE THE WIND

We may color the green of a blade of grass
Hear winds rustle through the trees
Watch artists paint pictures on canvas
Listen to roar of waves on the sea.

See a kite flying high in the air
Help a child hold the string.
Look for birds meeting in treetops
All those are beautiful things.

Travel on highways many a mile
From mountains to valleys descend
Trying to fly where earth meets sky
Is like trying to capture the wind.

Simple things in life can bring much joy
Really why should we pretend
Find gold at the end of a rainbow
I'd rather try capturing the wind.

So I watch the talented artist
Give thanks, God is my friend
Men may live on the moon someday
But they cannot capture the wind.

EYES

With eyes to see
Hands to touch
How can one say
That's not so much.

ITS LONELY

It's lonely not having someone
Sit beside me when a problem arises
Needing attention
Its then I realize more time
I should be spending
Helping ease the pain of one less fortunate
Knowing all the while that love, hope
And inspiration will heal the agony of defeat.
In doing for others I forget my own feelings
which were minor all the time.

Maybe I should do tomorrow
What was neglected yesterday
Failing to share in time of sorrow
Taking extra time to pray.

Because somewhere someone is lonesome
Wishing, hoping for a friend
Could be a lonesome traveler
Looking for his journeys end.

Things I do can be worthwhile
On this I make a bet
It will bring me happiness
And there is no regret.

LUCKY

I sit and think that somewhere
Someone might be in need
So taking out a minute
I say a prayer and plead.

Telling people who are lonely
Please no do not wear a frown
God has a way of knowing
When your smile is upside down.

Ask Him how very fortunate
Or lucky can you be
You've lived another day
My friend. pray on bended knee.

MEANING

What are kind thoughts
Cheerful greetings
Friendly handclasps
Joy filled meetings
Beautiful memories silver and gold
Seeing a new life begin to unfold..

CLOSE OF DAY

Happiness that lingers
At the close of day
Is knowing that you helped
Someone along the way.

ANTIQUE PICTURE FRAME

While looking through the attic
Among things of yesteryear
Memories returned to haunt me
Bringing back smiles and tears.

Remembering good times we had
Our lives not known for fame
I found something to cherish always
Pictured in an antique frame.

Hanging in a dusty corner
Where no one seemed to care
Was this heirloom most beautiful
And a couple seated there.

Standing silent for some minutes
With trembling hands and head bent low
Beside me you were whispering
As years pass our love will grow.

The picture frame I dusted gently
To live those years again
Still the love has never faded
Neither has the antique frame.

SEEDS

Wake up to see the morning come
As though it were your last
Being thankful for yesterdays
To remember the past.

Tomorrow we might gain new friends
Help doing a few good deeds
Sharing and caring always
We must plant some extra seeds.

Of love for life eternal
Without agony and pain
Give someone inspiration
Let's not sit and complain.

Knowledge comes from learning
Prayer is helpful when
From the beginning of day to ending
We whisper our last amen.

EIGHTY ONE

It's Christmas time in eighty-one
May you be blessed today
With my wish for a bountiful harvest
Of souls who have gone astray.

Children's eyes will sparkle
Seeing trees with tinsel bright
My hope all homes will glisten
With love this glorious night.

WISHES

Have you ever wished to visit
In lands across the sea
Studying the culture
Wishing all were trouble free.

A million times I must have said
I wish, an inexpensive pleasure
Then realize selfishness
There is much to treasure.

Health, happiness, religion of my choice
Friends, family and relation
All the food I need to neat
All cause for celebration.

Oh sure, I get discouraged
Which is human nature
Then I dream of foreign lands
My fantasies to recapture.

Dream on you fool, keep wishing
When they are fulfilled
Please pass along the recipe
It's better than a pill
Wish, a dream must never die
Don't spoil the joy of living
Everyone has imagination
Be understanding and forgiving.

A FORTUNE

My dreams are worth a fortune
Can't be sold at any price
Sharing them with someone a pleasure
Is really twice as nice.

Not seek gold at the rainbow
Would never be an aim in life
A friendship to treasure
Could mean a full measure
Easing trouble and strife.

I would hold them close in my arms
Take away anger and pain
Open the door to happiness
Help someone live again.

Much can be done for a neighbor
Or visiting a lonesome friend
Hours will pass more quickly
Giving joy until the days end.

May I reach out, hold your hand
Forget problems in the past
Unless each can be forgiving
The agony will last.

SMILE

THE DAY I SAW YOU SMILE AGAIN
I KNOW YOU WERE READY TO LIVE
FORGETTING THE PAIN SOMEONE CAUSED
BEING WILLING TO FORGIVE.

DISCOVERY

Watch as the moonbeams
Gaze at the stars
A land of enchantment
This world of ours.

Trade life for a fortune
No my foolish one
Storing up pleasures
Is much more fun.

Ski on the mountains
Sail the oceans of blue
Share love and laughter
With someone waiting for you.

Leave no time for tears
Give of your time
Discovery in doing
Returns riches sublime.

"Hello", a greeting
Spoken many times a day
Might bring cheer to someone near
Or loved one far away.

Write it in a letter
Say it o'er the phone
Help the day pass quickly
For one living all alone.

BEING YOU

There are many things in life
Including birds and bees
One of the most beautiful
Is all the flowering trees.

Happy children at their play
Whether home or in my pool
Hoping they will not forget
Learning the golden rule.

Making our land one of the best
You will ever find
A reason life is beautiful
When we have peace of mind.

Be gracious just by being you
Enjoy living, it's so great
When an occasion presents itself
We all go celebrate.

THEIR DAY

Each day of life given to me
Is really appreciated
May I return a gift to you
I am dedicated.

Telephone someone dear
Make their day with love enfold
I can't mend heartache
Try again I'm told.

SING

The day passed quickly
I heard you doing many things
Listening I wondered
What made your heart sing.

Picking up your rosary
You said a little prayer
It was wonderful
Knowing you were there.

CARDINAL

The bird outside my window
A Cardinal with lofty crown
Whistling to his lady friend
Picking up crumbs from the ground.

He is warning her of Tigger and Midnight
Our neighbors cats on the prowl
I really don't mind them being around
Except nights when they howl.

There is also a cottontail
Living on the south hill
I was afraid he might get caught
But starlings give warning that chill.

Winter has come I see them no more
Leaves fell and blew away
When spring returns, they too return
To brighten a dreary day.

A THOUGHT

Wanting you near most of the time
Gazing at stars up above
Thoughts came to me, why should there be
Such pain and heartache in love.

I want you by my side
Each hour of every day
Wishing nothing but the best in life
Remembering in some small way.

SYMBOL OF LOVE

Like a trail that leads to somewhere
Or road that goes to the sea
You whispered of love and promised
Together we always would be.

Walking 'neath trees where birds nested
Beaches where sandpipers roam
Memories will linger like the rings on my finger
Until you are safe at home.

Rings on my finger symbol of love
May each day be sunny and bright
God in his glory is watching
Each time I whisper goodnight.

SOMEONE TO LOVE

There is someone for each to love
This has been told in the stars
Somebody to hold you very close
In all the lonely hours.

Seems I waited a lifetime
Wondering where my someone could be
Now there is no room for fear
Because my someone found me.

Don't turn away from tomorrow
That might be the day
When the one you're searching for
Appears to brighten your day.

Since I found somebody to love
We share a lifetime of bliss
Remembering it all happened
After only one kiss.

The one to thank is watching
Caring for me I know
Giving protection when needed
Lighting my pathway to show.

That I must bow down my head
Thanking our god on high
When we find someone and are grateful
Happiness he will never deny.

ENTERTAINING

Not a person of worldly fame
I like just being me
An ordinary human
Best for all you see.

I like entertaining folks
It takes no special mood
A simple kind of living
To cook and serve good food.

My pleasures were multiplied
When you came to call that day
We talked of many things
About friends who moved away.

Some said how surprised they were
When we moved from the city
To live in a small village
But admitted it was pretty.

Liking it here, we plan to stay
Feel proud to be a part
Of folks who seem so genuine
Act like you have a heart.

Whenever you pay a visit
Hope you will agree
While living in a village small
We still entertain graciously.

HOW ABOUT

The plans you made for tomorrow

Then suddenly realizing

That was yesterday!

APPRECIATE

Don't hesitate to appreciate
The greatest gift God extends
Just believe tomorrow holds
A future filled with friends.

BE QUIET

Did you ever think asking a child to be quiet

Would be like telling birds not to fly.

SWEET NOTHING

Whispering a sweet nothing is
More profitable than
A rash of ugly words.

AWAKENING

The sun awakens the morning
It's like a beautiful birth
Makes us realize we're living
In the greatest place on earth.

Having things to do makes me happy
With little time for tears
Glorifying in the knowledge
God can brush away all fears.

Even though the snow is falling
Easter very close at hand
Seems all through life we're asking
For peace in this wonderful land.

The little rabbit is happy
As he runs along the fence
There is beauty surrounding us
Let not minds grow dense.

Awaken to the glory
See another wondrous morn
Giving thanks to the almighty
Being glad we were born.

The sun awakes, another dawning
It is Easter, He is risen
May prayers of all the faithful
Help erase what was his prison.

TEN FEET TALL

Not a queen of any land
My chance for that is small
When I can be helpful
I feel 'bout ten feet tall.

Good health is mine, a lovely home
Grandchildren number give
Another reason to be happy
It's great being alive.

I work in town part time each day
Help anyone in need
A millionaire to never be
Still I'm going to succeed.

Give the simple things in life
A visit with good friends
If hurting someone, may I please
Have a chance to make amends.

Happy yes but not a queen
I reign at thirty-nine Crestview Drive
Whenever you wish please pay a call
I am there from nine to five.

PLEASE

I say life is wonderful
Seeing you begins my day
Sharing your knowledge as usual
Gives strength in a special way.

THE WEAK

Dream on you fool
There is no cost
Without that dream
All hope is lost.

Beware of thoughts
That let you stray
Seek, find the good
Along the way.

You're given a chance
Try and pursue
The best in life
Will follow you.

Don't say I can't
Give yourself a chance
Encouragement
Will help you advance.

A little laughter
When day is through
Could be the best
Medicine for you.

Then just before you
Try to sleep
Add some prayers
God hears the weak.

SEARCH FOR FAME

You'll find heartache and loneliness
In frantic search for fame
Remember that all need love
Life is not a wayward game.

Some sadness for each happiness
Pain for all mankind
Riches may buy many things
Joy comes from a peaceful mind.

If we avoid all temptation
Live by the golden rule
There would be less heartache
For those you try to fool.

You think you know the answers now
Look not for faults because
Remember in that search for fame
There's more to life than applause.

UNTIL

I did not smile today until
A bird perched on my windowsill
The cardinal with bright red crown
Left no reason to show a frown
This is known to everyone
Look and see the shining sun.

1983

It is spring again in eighty-three
Robins are on the wing
New life has been given
To every living thing.

REASONS FOR LOVE

Heartbreak I felt when you left me
Even made the stars dim above
Seems life is empty for me
I have no reason for love.

Shall I go away not bother
The strange life you want to live
Like a butterfly chasing a rainbow
I will try and forgive.

If ever we meet on the corner
My thoughts remind me of
A long time ago when you left me
Taking my reason for love.

There always will be a season for love
Mine stopped when you went away
Praying someday I find life can be kind
Sending a reason for love my way.

WISHING

Peace of mind to all mankind
If I may be so bold
Life has been a joy to me
Although now I'm growing old.

Quiet living brings contentment
Showered with goodwill
May all prayers be answered
And all dreams fulfilled.

SAINT PAT

There is a day to celebrate
March seventeen is the reason
Comes once every year
During the Lenten season.

Have some fun do the Irish jig
Wear a shamrock and green hat
You can be as Irish as Patty's pig
On the feast day of Saint Pat.

GOOD THINGS

Let not your life be saddened
By someone who made you cry
Seems they should be pitied
You need not wonder why.

Think of all the good things
In many that you meet
They help erase evil feelings
Cause you heart to skip a beat.

The smile and hand that's offered
When they see you come in sight
A beautiful thing to remember
Everyday from morn 'til night.

Many folks are unhappy
As they travel down life's road
Showing them some kindness
Is returned a hundred fold.

FEBRUARY

Seems like only yesterday

I tried to write a song

Labored o'er the words so much

Gave feeling I belonged.

Among the weary travelers

Who fail to keep in touch

I take my pen in hand again

My mind is in quandary

Could be I cannot concentrate

In the month of February.

Now my heart is listless

Because the sun lost its glow

Memories come back to taunt me

Are my footsteps getting slow.

I look forward always

Never grieving about the past

February does not mean forever

And happiness will surely last.

GRUBS

It's great to see the shining sun
On all the trees and shrubs
I like the bees and birds that sing
But have no use for those darn grubs.

Out comes the spray can and the hose
I'm thinking after a while
That sun could be hot enough
To cook them charcoal style.

CLOUDS

Treasure each day from beginning
As you rise from wonderful sleep
Mysterious things are happening
Memories to cherish and keep.

The day will pass more quickly
Doing things you love
Share a smile with a lonely child
Watch clouds floating above.

Rock-a-bye dream of sweet things
In the afternoon don't you peek
Rise from your nap, watch the day
Start putting the sun to sleep.

Earth meets sky in the evening
Soon all the shadows creep
Day ended too soon, gave way to the moon
After putting the sun to sleep.

ENJOY

I like to roam the highways
Enjoying this glorious land
Still I find enchantment
Reaching out a helping hand.

LONG AGO

Memories are what dreams are made of
We keep them close to our heart
Dreams make life worth living
From them I will not part.

They bring back childhood things
That happened long ago
Puppy love of teenage years
Many tears were shed I know.

Memories fill the lonely hours
Of people growing old
What if they are repeated
When often times they're told.

What is memory without a dream
Being told a mystery
Something to last a lifetime
And part of history.

BE MY GUEST

Seeing you smile makes me happy
May I ask this request
If sometime you're invited
Would you be my guest.

I like your sincerity
When you offer your hand
But please don't break a promise
Not easy for me to understand.

KAREN

Time to croon a happy tune
For such a charming girl
She is our Miss America
Karen sets each heart a whirl.

A crown she enjoys wearing
This little one so bold
With brown eyes that really sparkle
Yet only three years old.

Many pleasures she gives us
Every single day she grows
Trying to see into everything
Standing on tiptoes.

There are beautiful children everywhere
Giving joy beyond all measure
But Karen is my grandchild
A life to really treasure.

SACRED HEART CONVENT

A place where quiet and beauty reigns
There precious moments must dwell
A home of love and understanding
Each doing their best to fill.

Pleasures to each who reside there
Knowing laughter might ease pain
This being my first visit
They ask, please return again.

ALTAR OF LOVE

Humbly we ask for your mercy
Showered on us from above
May we ever be worthy
Kneel at your altar of love.

Oft times I might grow weary
As the days pass by
I should stop and thank the master
On his blessings I rely.

He helps when we are worthy
Will not neglect us you see
With all knowledge of living
A solid foundation is He.

Humbly we beg your helping hand
Shower blessing from above
May mankind be granted forgiveness
Kneeling at your altar of love.

THE LAST AMEN

Ave Maria so profoundly we sing
Kneeling before you the angelus ring
Sancta Maria your blessings extend
Throughout life until the last amen.

Many times I have been blessed
Receiving forgiveness on each request
With your intercession I will not sin
Asking to be worthy until the last amen.

WONDERS

Wonders of living
In children abound
Springtime its kites
In winter they're found
Sledding down hills
Much fun and laughter
It's great for them
Not knowing what will come after.

Wonders of teenage
When things seem grand
You hold the future
Of this world in your hand.

Education and knowledge
Surround you each day
While you enjoy life
The American way.

If you marry when older
Anxiety you face
Wishing the glories of childhood
You might replace.

Wonderful times lots of good will
Now hours of working you fill
Day comes, thoughts of tomorrow
When pain you might bear
If only life was enjoyed
Without shedding a tear.

EARTH

Just give the best
To the land of your birth
Work, relax and enjoy
This good planet earth.

PEACE CHARLIE COBB

Why did our hearts feel lonely
When God took you away
Leaving many thoughts behind
Had we hurt in any way.

We had dreams that someday
Lives together we might spend
With a smile we remember
We had you for a friend.

May you be happy in heaven
A place we each hope to go
You were a beautiful person
Seeing you made our eyes glow.

Thinking about you in daily prayers
Our faith each day to increase
Knowing you made life worthwhile
May you have eternal peace.

NO SUN

A dreary day
No sun I see and yet
I feel God smiles on me
He gave me life
He lets me live
And when I sin
He will forgive.

BUILDERS

Look up smile and see
The pleasure of those men on bridges high
Crossing o'er the Halifax River
Enjoying height like birds that fly.
Wondering as I walk along
Wind whispering in the sand
It's great to be alive
In this glorious land
Today I want to think about
Tomorrow's come around
Remembering yesterday
I watch you build the bridge
We use when homeward bound.

LOVINGLY

Loving you in many ways
From day to set of sun
If you think of me
Wonder just how often
I tell you lovingly
You have a gentle smile
Since meeting some time ago
My days seem more worthwhile
I want you for a sweet heart
Bold as this might be
Please believe when I say
This is said honestly.

SECRET

I don't mind gray skies
Or any other hue
Wishing just to get along
Really this is true.

So what if we act foolish
Sometimes get to feeling blue
Just want to tell you baby
I'm bad when I'm with you.

When two people fall in love
Saying you're the only and only
There will be better times ahead
No more feeling lonely.

Come and visit I will tell
All my secret wishes
If I cook, you stay around
And we'll do the dishes.

Never let the lonesome bug
Get you down and out
Pick up the phone and call
Relieve you mind of doubt.

I will try to show
My love for you is true
Then I hope you realize
I'm only bad with you.

IF

If in doubt forget it
If not, you might regret it.

MY TRIBUTE

He lived here, walked among people of the land
Here he lived leaving a heritage grand
We honor him with loyalty and pride
The man, Lincoln known far and wide.

He lived here many years ago
Born in Kentucky a truth we all know
Went to Petersburg, New Salem has won fame
There lives a legend long to remain.

He lived here, capitol of our state
Worked, served, built a home
To people here a native son
Went to be President in Washington
Here he lived still many come
Visit his home, pay tribute at the tomb
Listen to the age old story
Then to New Salem, roam the territory.
Our state's age reaches plus one hundred fifty
A place I belong
Located in the heart of the U.S.A.
Seldom do we hear the state's song.

We have rivers that flow gently
Our harvests, best in the land
Also forests and wild life found here
And Illinois lakes are grand.

WINTER

Winter the season that follows the fall
Time we hope snowflakes will call
With icicles hanging from rooftops and trees
Time for mufflers, ice skates and skis.

Season of winter tingling of toes
Frostbite that tickles like Rudolph's red nose
Beautiful scenery on hillside and stream
Things we see in a wonderful dream

I like the season that makes children sing
Quickens the heartbeat of all
Candy cane fairyland, snow birds on the wing
What is winter until snowflakes fall.

December's joys abound to surround us
At Christmas church bells will ring
Trumpets will sound the world around
To celebrate the birthday of our King.

SPARE MOMENT

It will soon be a year of remembering
Since God came and took you away
My thoughts are with you darling
Each time I stop to pray.

If there is a spare moment
Of time in your heavenly home
Please think of the good times
My prayers are yours alone.

TREAT FOR MAN

Have you traveled across the skyways
A treat for any man
Still the great expanse of highways
Lure me like a gypsy clan.

They wind around each other
Oft times four levels high
Buckle up let's go my friend
Find where earth meets sky.

We live along a highway
Not known from coast to coast
The traffic does not bother me
What intrigues me the most?

Trucks, cars, vans and busses
With colors of every hue
Taking children to school
People to some rendezvous.

Pick up a paper you can read
Travel this road it's terrific
After only two thousand miles
View the blue Pacific.

If you feel a wee bit inclined
Driving around for pleasure
Stay off those superhighways
Less traveled ones you'll treasure.

FROM DENNY

How come grandma that you go to church everyday.
Is it because you need time to drive your sins away.

THANKSGIVING

Working all day without much pay
Hours from seven to seven
Preparing so folks can celebrate
The feast day of Thanksgiving.

Hams to bake, turkeys to roast
Steaks, ribs and chops
Oysters, eggs, ducks and geese
Really make us hop.

Please wait on me I am nest
With patience we must serve
Owning your own business
Takes a world of nerve.

Well this day will soon be over
Tho tired, life is worth living
Many may not be around another year
So let's celebrate Thanksgiving.

GREATNESS

Travel on a highway or down a dusty road
Lift your thoughts
Let cheerfulness
Lighten up the load.

Share a handshake or a smile
Listen to the sounds of earth
As sunshine casts a shadow
You might hear the children's mirth

Having been to Puerto Rico
Hawaii and the Virgin Isles
Visited Florida and California
Where climates are warm and mild.

Seen wild ocean waves at sunset
Viewed their calm at early dawn
These places hold great meaning
Land of free where I was born.

We have mountains and deserts
Farmlands where the mighty harvests grow
Reaping grains to feed the nation
A world that's on the go.

This land of heritage and knowledge
When one listens, sure to learn
That the right to keep our freedom
A lesson taught well learned.

Let we not forget the Master
Who promised anytime we fall

He will raise us up, give us strength
Because love will conquer all.

MOTHER'S POEM 1929

Last night while I lay sleeping
Tho lying wide awake
I wondered if the ice cream
And pickles gave you the tummy ache.

It was midnight by the town clock
Not an Ashland cop in sight
They must have been on coffee break
Which is ten times a night!

Going to take a stroll downtown
I suffered quiet a fright
The barkeep in the tavern
Was Lorna in red tights.

She was singing happily
The latest song she'd heard
With a voice like a canary
The song, "Bye, Bye Blackbird."

Right now I'm peeling peaches
Underneath the apple tree
And soon I'll pick strawberries
In the sand beside the sea

Little Bobbie has the pink eye
He is here at home
I wish he would behave himself
So I can write this poem.

Now Jack I hope you enjoy these words
About people that you know

I better get this posted
Pony Express is very slow.

ROOM FOR ALL

Not a teacher of history
Nor English literature
No good at mathematics
Can't play an overture.

Used to fly an airplane
When I was quite young
Gave that up to have children
With lullabys to be sung.

I know there is room for all
Doing anything if we try
Reaching the peak of contentment
Is easy, need ask why.

Loving a beautiful thing
Should always give a thrill
Climb the heights of enchantment
Don't stand at the foot of the hill.

Stretch, grasp the hand of a stranger
Extended for help on the way
Travel the highway to knowledge
Listen and obey.

There is room for all
Both great and small
Look around you will find
Happiness comes from doing
Good deeds for mankind.

TRICIA

Bundle of joy with eyes of blue
Chases all cares away
Golden haired little Tricia
Mimics each word we say.

She will charm you if weary
Cause you to smile tho sad
She brings happiness to each
Sister, brothers, mom and dad.

A delight when she comes to visit
Grandpa, grandma and Don
Never quiet for a minute
Runs like a marathon.

Need not be lonesome with Tricia
Though the world seems upside down
When she visits it's wonderful
And erases any cause for a frown.

AFFAIRS OF THE HEART

You 're the dream I hold in my heart
Will you belong to me
Although many miles apart
You hold the lock and key.

Dawns the morn a new day
You'll learn how soon my love
I appreciate each day of living
Accepting strength from above.

I need not be a gypsy
Roaming the countryside
Never allow idle moments
Must keep the mind occupied.

Affairs of heart forgiving
A harvest reaped in gold
Doing for others the message
Many times over we are told.

Never being thoughtless
Holding on to a dream
Building a stairway to happiness
Filled with vivacious esteem.

Learn being patient with life
Living each day at best
Your love was gained my darling
God answers enormous requests.

DAYS OF SPRING

Days of spring mean everything
To those in love
Awakening starts foolish hearts
Coo like a dove.

Blustering winds life begins
To show on trees
Wild flowers bloom every soon
Come honey bees.

Mornings come the fog hangs low
Shrouding hill and vale
The sun will shine words will rhyme
Like a fairytale.

Watch a stream pin your dream
On white clouds drifting by
Hear my love echoing
Never let you cry.

Days pass along, sing a song
Walking hand in hand
A honeymoon some day soon
Is our plan.

It's good to know you love me
Someone heard my plea
May we keep the days of spring
A lasting memory.

REMIND ME GOD

Remind me God with I'm alone
And feel in deep despair
Let not my ailing heart forget
You hear every prayer.

Remind me God no matter what
I do or fail to do
You won't abandon anyone
Whose faith in you is true.

Let not my eyes be sightless
When some folly I commit
Help me to regret the wrong
I must atone for it.

Inspire me to believe
Put fear upon the shelf
Allow no twinge of jealousy
When someone else has wealth.

You gave us life and we should
Make the most of each day
Never get so involved
We find no time to pray.

Control temper, be more kind
Have courage to go on
Remind me God, I heed your help
To view another dawn.

CHATHAM, ILLINOIS

Many things are written about
Place in the land
More than twenty bear this name
Ours the one that's grand.

No shopping centers, nightclubs
Parking problems not yet
Square dancers can entertain
Are we proud, you bet.

We have finest churches, modern schools
Educating girls and boys
You'll find us located
In central Illinois.

There is a bank to store the wealth
Post office, bowling alley too
One is great, the other fun
The mail must go through.

A super market, drug store, auctioneers who chant
Hardware store, lumberyard, manufacturing plant
Realtors, restaurants, even beauty parlors
Fraternal organizations assisting worthy scholars

Service stations, pizza places and community hall
Fire house, library, antiques, that's not all
Repair shops, friendly people have garage sales
Tavern to quench your thirst with finest beers and ales.

We won't take fame from any city
Ours just a village we think mighty pretty

Country homes, beautiful people, girls and boys
I'm bragging 'bout the place I live, Chatham, Illinois.

MUSIC IN MY HEART

The wheels are slowly turning
To the music in my heart
Seems just looking around me
There is magic to impart.

Why not help someone in need
A problem they must face
Happiness is found in doing
Sharing an embrace.

Don't pout about the small things
Shake them off when they arise
You must take, along with giving
Aid the one less wise.

Stretch a hand in friendship
Even when the heart knows pain
Life you see is worth living
You might not have this chance again.

To view the sunrise in the morning
The dew, the rain or snow
Life like a burning candle
Will sometime lose its glow.

Try each day a little harder
No need to show defeat
When then sharing laughter
Feel life is complete.

SPLENDOR

The moon shines bright
On winters snow and casts
A glow of loveliness
On earth's bare trees
Then gives way to spring
When everything turns green
Birds, sing, buds break forth in splendor.
Then summer comes and flowers bloom
The glorious time of awakening
For all living things
How wonderful to be in love
Have a beautiful outlook on life
Being honestly appreciative of
Knowing without friends
There would be little need for existence.
The beauty that surrounds us each day
Is like a blanket of life
Waiting to be unfolded
Then grasping the magnificent
Feeling of being alive.

THE HILL

I climbed the hill to happiness
What I found you wouldn't guess
My dream became reality
You climbed the hill to sit with me.

WORK OF ART

Many lonely hours I've spent
Since we have been apart
Sands of time leave etchings
Like a noble work of art.

Look up at the vastness
A plane streaks cross the sky
Know without the hand of God
Not even birds could fly.

After storms watch the rainbow
Water glistening on the land
Thirsty earth was gladdened
The struggling farmer clasps his hand.

Long days pass more quickly
Listen, I will tell you why
The day of parting gone forever
A work of art, the butterfly.

Flits around from flower to flower
Adding beauty to the land
Birds in radiant color
Captured by the artists hand.

Learn of glory everywhere
Etchings are a part
The chance to be living
Enjoying the Master's work of art.

TO THERESA

A friend asked me recently
If the past you could live over
What did you miss at any time
Think of yesterdays they cover
Dream of all tomorrows
Relive journeys you took
Leaving behind the sorrows
Not written in a memory book.

Things I remember most
Were the lunches we enjoyed
Many times you were not present
Because you were still employed.

Those days bring back many thoughts
Your wedding days and such
Children brought much happiness
Raised with your tender touch.

Sadness came along and yes
Gave pain and bitter loss
Bridges do not last forever
Rivers do on which we cross.

You have suffered much heartache
For loves ones called by God
Wondering when would it end
As on the earth we trod.
You have been a gallant soldier
Through the years and ages

Faith has kept you beautiful
So as we turn the pages

We pray for you each passing day
Dearest Theresa understand
When we feel, what's the use
God holds out His hand.

So as the days pass by
We ask the master and implore
Dear God help Theresa this we pray
Open her get well door.

LASTING LOVE

Whispering breeze across the seas
Beneath a pale blue sky
Fly away to swing and sway
Without a sigh.

The surf will roll we will stroll
Along the sparkling sand
A dream come true you whispered
Hold my hand.

You came to me with love
Bright as the stars above
Saying words so gentle
Like orchids beauty rare.

Strolling neath the moonlight
These words to me were said
Our love will be lasting
Like the famous diamond head.

I am home from the sea
Where the fragrance of Plumeria
No longer wakens me
Here to stay, know someday
Remember with a sigh
To never forget Hawaii
While life passes by.

SMALL BOY AT MY SIDE

To Don

Mom I didn't mean to bother
Or cause you any worry
Although when I ask a question
Seems you're always in a hurry.

Why not relax, slow down a while
Take time out to rest
The days seems so very short
When answering my requests.

Hey mom I need some suntan oil
Are my sneakers clean
Is it necessary staying home
Insisting would be mean.

Some of the fellows will be by
Collier, Howard, Tom and Ron
We thought a swim would be the thing
When the temp one hundred one.

Since growing up, work each day
Time has gone so fast
No regrets at all the company
Just helping out when asked.

You thought I was short tempered
But failed to realize
None but the best was ever wished
Along with clear blue skies.

Soon you will travel all around
I take each day in its stride
Looking at yesterday it seems
You were a small boy at my side.

OVER MY SHOULDER

You may look over my shoulder
I have memories to share
When you hear me sing
May it bring
Happiness to chase away care.

Shy when I sang in public
Yet trying so had to be
Grown up like all the others
Wishing my life were free.

When looking over my shoulder
Times I received a scare
Like a will-of-the-wisp
Out of the mist
You were standing there.

What fun to have been a dancer
On a stairway that led to the sky
Now that I'm older
Someone's on my shoulder
So I croon a lullaby.

Someday I hope you listen
Maybe sometime sing
If looking over my shoulder
Keep remembering
Please look over your shoulder
At the glories you might share
Tho we part, you have my heart
I'm leaving in your care.

RITA

Seems many years ago
And yet quite recently
Rita was a child herself
Sitting on our knee.
Now she has give
Two girls, three boys
And constantly
Pick up toys, still
No frown comes on her face.
She cooks, scrubs
And cleans the place
Not little angels we agree
This holy terror five
Can entertain you
With their ambitious drive.
Hey, can I do this or that
Oh, what are you doing now
Grandpa went to sleep again
Can we eat anyhow.
Grandma can we stay again
Must we go home with mom
We cherish the day
Of small grandchildren
For soon will be grown and gone.

UNKNOWN

Thought I never see you often
My love just seems to grow
Tell me did you forget
What was promised long ago.

Loving the little things
Tenderness that was shown
Reminds me, always care
Though I remain unknown.

PLASTIC CARD

I shall go to town today
To do a little shopping
Buy a dress and some new shoes
Its better than bar hopping.
Everything so expensive
Ready made or by the yard
Although the cost seems reasonable
When I use that plastic card.

ENOUGH

In a million smiles
There are a million miles
Enough for a lifetime of pleasure
When reaching a goal
The memory you can treasure.

LIVING THINGS

Living to see the shining sun
Enjoying a cloudy day
Listen to children singing
They go along the way.

Flower buds are bursting
Gloom is not for lovely things
Smiles can bring happiness
Harsh words only sting.

We need the rain, a blessing
Warmth of days in spring
Need love for one another
To you I'm offering.

The glories of all living things
Filled with joy and laughter
Because we never know how soon
Comes the calling of the Master.

NOT TRUE

Am I falling for you darling
Really I'm not sure
When undecided my mom used to say
Castor oil is the cure.

TRYING

I sat down and wrote
A song some years ago
But no one would listen
Guess I better try something else
Like watching stars
As they glisten
Songs have been written
Through the ages
Gaining success a different story
That old cliché try again
Is as staunch as
Flying Old Glory.
Maybe I'll try again
To grab the brass ring, and yet
If my luck doesn't change by tomorrow
There are memories to never forget.

STAR OF HOPE

Tenderness not forgotten
When doing for mankind
Because after most stars
Have gone to sleep
One of hope will ever shine.

SADNESS

There will be sadness
If you ever leave
You caused my sun to shine
When tired and weary.
Help we seek, the Master
Is never unkind.

He knew when the burden was heavy
Temptation stood in the way
Quietly saying have patience
At times we are all afraid
Who wants to face the world alone
Words so often we repeat
Please dear Load, hear these prayers
Offering laid at your feet.

I OWE

Thank you God for everyday
The blessings you bestow
My life, a gift that came from you
To all success I owe.

GRANDCHILDREN

Grandchildren are a joy to me
Joe and I have five in number
Always noisy while at play
Quiet when they slumber.

Growing up a pain to them
Especially if grandparents fuss
Just where in the world would they be
If there weren't any of us.

To grandma and grandpa everywhere
Look forward to each celebration
Leave memories that show you cared
As they branch out across the nation.

Show you care, they won't forget
To send greetings once in awhile
They will remember the good times
When you watched them with a smile.

TIME

Time passes quickly as we know
Life puts us to the test
Better be a clown than wear a frown
Enjoy each moment with zest.

WE CARE

Hearing the bells
Seeing the smiles
People not afraid to pray
Kneeling before the crib
Where the infant lay.

Heard the songs about peace on earth
We care knowing only too well
Somewhere in this great big world
There was the bursting of a shell.

Now silently we wait
Bells at midnight
A greeting may we cheer
For those who came to church
Hope to return this time next year.

Our land has much to offer
Each hour living pray
Ours the gift of knowing
God gave us the right of way.

DENNY

Well little man move over
Wipe that frown from your face
A little sister has arrived
Taking what used to be your place.

Talking much you might say
What's going on around here today
Quit looking at that baby new
Come on somebody, tie my shoe.

Why the heck can't you see
I'm still around here, golly gee
Get me a drink, do you suppose
Someone can help me
With my clothes.

Remember I was little too
You used to look at me and coo
With Rick, Tim and Denny ... me
That's still more boys
Than girls you see.

I must grow up and learn real fast
Talk and do the things I'm asked
My big ideas will sprout you'll see
People will stop ignoring me.

FAREWELL JACK

Don would give Jack a kiss
Use the dryer after a bath
He sure never caused a problem
Only when thunder sounded a blast.

Will we ever forget our Jack
As days and weeks go by
Thinking of him is painful
To be brave we must try.

Don loved Jack so very much
I know his pain will stay
Trying to keep busy
Doesn't make memories go away.

Jack, no one will replace you
I am lonesome and alone
Part of me went with you
When you left number ten your home.

Goodbye again my little friend
As each day passes by
I walk around the house and pool alone
Trying to keep my eyes dry.

I'll love you to my journeys end
You were a blessed true blue friend.

Love, Mom

24 APRIL 2005

BEAUTY

You have to work at friendship
In a garden filled with flowers
Unless you want the weeds to grow
And spoil the many hours
You spent in weeding, feeding
Those tender little seeds
Like a moment taken
Doing kindly deeds.

We can't live on make-believe
Although our dreams add beauty
Sharing secrets with someone
Brings happiness not duty.

May we let friendship grow
Reaching out our hand
Extending to one in need
Across this wondrous land.

Plant some flowers, show some love
Learn too be forgiving
Even though times we hurt
It's great to be living.

Need some help, ask
God will hear your plea
Smile to show how graciously
He cared and I agree.

A TRIBUTE TO PRESIDENT JOHN FITZGERALD KENNEDY

The smile that embraced a nation
A friendly hand clasp I'm told
Was the man we knew as president
With a heart so big and bold.

He love the land, the deep blue sea
Traveled far and wide,
His greatest thought—the peace he sought
To keep all nations free with pride.

To help each loving mother's son
His goal, that peace be known
His hope, their life—no grief nor strife
The seeds of hatred never sown.

God gives and yet he took away
A man so daring, brave and strong
Who did not sway at close of day
But gained the strength to carry on.

He left so many memories
His work, his job well done
While his loving family
Have lost a cherished one.

He had no fear to hide his life
Beneath a bubbled glass
No thought one evil troubled mind
Would be in the crowd as he rode past.

[TRIBUTE TO PRESIDENT JOHN FITZGERALD KENNEDY—continued]

The tears I shed when first they said,
Our President, this man we knew
As friend to all even on foreign soil *was dead*
His life passed in review.

We know the guardian angel watches
Over loved ones lift behind
We pray each day in our own way
To understand with peace of mind.

Now as we look across our land
And try to keep in stride
We hope that all, both great and small
Will make his plans, his hopes, their guide.

I hope someday that I may see
In Arlington, the lasting flame
I'll kneel while there to say a prayer
For a man, a hero and martyr
God grant his name
Be held by all in high esteem
Have mercy on the one who shattered his dream.

THE TRIBUTE

A year has passed yet in my heart
The pain still lingers on
Those shots were heard around the world
That took a beloved son.

How great a man this country had
His willingness was shown
He gave as many soldier have
His life, now we must carry on.

Even little children feel
They knew this president
His death to them caused many questions
Why a life so good was spent.

My memory will never dim
Of this friendly brilliant man
The whole world was reaching out
To grasp his extended hand.

May the blessings of a better life
Grant him peace, keep his loved ones safe
Lest they have cause for alarm
Free from worry and fear of harm.

He traveled all around the world
Made friends a million fold
I will remember him in prayer
This man was good, with heart of gold.

[THE TRIBUTE—continued]

I feel his death has kept us free
The fighting from our shore
Take him to heaven with you God
Keep him safe and secure.

May we not pass judgment on
The one with such an evil mind
Let us more worthy be each day
His agony he will find.

So lift you voices sing aloud
Your blessings will be plenty
Be glad we had a president
As fine as John F. Kennedy.

This tribute on the first anniversary
of the death of
President John Fitzgerald Kennedy
Written by Frances Helen Kunzweiler

HOW GREAT

It was just two years ago
And long I will remember
Our nation was in deep mourning
We had lost the greatest member.

The people do not soon forget
His gentle smiling face
His voice a guidepost for
The great United States.

Many loved ones this we know
Look back on that sad day
With tear dim eyes I'll bow my head
With humility to pray.

Will you forgive us please Dear Lord
Protect us if you can
Give peace of mind to everyone
Who loved this gracious man.

Let us be worthy each and all
For what this good man started
Side by side to live in pride
With hope for broken hearted.

Mothers, fathers, wives and children
As loved, serve throughout this land
To keep the war from our own shore
Though you must go to Viet Nam.

[HOW GREAT—continued]

I feel were he alive today
This thing called war would cease
Because foreign nations looked to him
As the leader seeking peace.

How great a man who never sought
Any fame or glory
His name will live forever in history
So all may know the story.

This tribute on the second anniversary
of the death of
President John Fitzgerald Kennedy
Written by Frances Helen Kunzweiler

HE KNOWS

Though memory sometimes dims the thought
Of this good man who had to fall
He faced this country's biggest problems
Then answered the Master's call.

We still wonder and always will
What made that man go mad
To be so ignorant in this world today
Is truly something very sad.

A monument you will see
When you visit Arlington
People go there everyday
To pray at dawn and setting sun.

The name of Dallas causes chills
In people young and old
A place I do not wish to visit
It would leave me sad and cold.

I feel that our former president
Knows the country is in a mess
Just recently we lost three space men
Now they too must know our distress.

These four had served their country well
And we must proceed I am told
Still their memories we do not erase
In loved ones, the country will remold.

[HE KNOWS—continued]

A pattern to be followed
Get someone to take each ones place
We know John F. Kennedy was the backbone
For the flight into space.

His belief in everyone, his joy in doing
Would not let him deter nor cease
He tried to find the answer
To an everlasting peace.

This tribute on the third anniversary
of the death of
President John Fitzgerald Kennedy
Written by Frances Helen Kunzweiler

THE GREATEST MAN I REMEMBER

A smile that gave us confidence as we watched
Across the country wide
His strength was great in every state
Each needed him to guide.

He went to foreign countries
Seeking the peace his only plan
The burden of the United States
Lay upon the shoulders of this great man.

His travels took him everywhere
Sometimes the pain he suffered with no complaint
Makes me feel how foolish some are
When they act like a saint.

This president I will remember
He gave much of his time
To seek peace for all the nations
Few men like him we ever find.

I am not ashamed by tears I shed
Whenever I recall
How we depended on this president
So our country would not fall.

His goal to be the best in everything
His cabinet appointees the bravest men
No matter what their politics
Both parties agreed they needed him.

[THE GREATEST MAN I REMEMBER—continued]

To Arlington someday I will go
And pay with great respect
A tribute to the man of men
Who worked so diligently
He gave his life, a gift from God
To keep our country free.

This tribute on the fourth anniversary
of the death of
President John Fitzgerald Kennedy
Written by Frances Helen Kunzweiler

THANK YOU JJ

Thank you JJ for caring about Jack
Especially your letter of consolation
We miss our little guy so very much
He was our inspiration.

Rising up early each morning
To take his usual walk
But when he'd see you in the evening
He knew Don would stop and talk.

Jack would recognize you in an instant
Even though you might be distant
He'd stare with his tail all wiggly
Stop and wait for your cookie.

He was my friend and companion
When Don would go on vacation
He was careful when meeting strangers
They could cause his vexation.

We have loving memories of Jack
Your thoughtful letter meant so much
I guess time heals all wounds
And friends like you and Ursula
Add special touch.

JANUARY 2005

Coming from Australia
The city of Perth
Where kangaroos are hopping
In their land of birth.

From Perth to Singapore
China on to Glasgow
Scotland, London England
To the USA in Orlando
Then from Florida to LA
On jets high in the sky
Their time in America too short
The days flew quickly by.

Stephanie and Richard
Came to see us that evening in January
With dad Jack came to visit
Our weather was contrary.

Visiting with Auntie Joan
And Uncle Charlie Cobb
Going to Disney, keeping busy
Shopping, what a glorious job.

Taking pictures, eating ice cream
They were here a couple years ago
Growing up beautiful and handsome
Full of pep to overflow

I imagine they kept dad busy
From the day they flew from Perth

To Scotland, England, then the USA
All great places on this earth.

Upon leaving Ormond Beach
On January thirty-one 2005
To Orlando then Los Angeles
Where fame and fortune always thrive.

FOR THE JOHN F. CLARKES

Perth in the country down under
Aberdeen a place of charm and wonder
Singapore such a business host in their nation
On to Glasgow to spend a wonderful vacation.
London, home of royalty and Big Ben
Orlando you must visit us again
Los Angeles, city of angels where stars shine
Hollywood, the film makers shrine.

Crossing many miles of skyways
Over oceans, rivers, earth
Seeing things for a memory book
A diary to read when they return to Perth.

Traveling is an education
Gain all the knowledge you can
Help yourself to life and loving
When visiting any land.

Carol and Kristine came later
To visit Auntie Joan and Uncle Charlie
Their visit was very short
But a good time was had and jolly.

Why is it time passes quickly
When we are away from home
Many more things we could do
If extra time to roam.

Joan is a real trooper
Charlie's illness has been rough
We keep them in our prayers

Asking God to lend a hand
To help us through and understand.

What is to be will be
Let us never give up hope
That each day will be better
As Joan continues to cope.

So Jack, Carol, Kristine, Richard, Stephanie
Each day say a tiny prayer
Auntie Joan's angel will hear you
And go with her everywhere.

A BUDDY

We lost our little salt and pepper Schnauzer
The best friend we ever had
A dog so kind and intelligent
We miss him and feel so very sad.

He belonged to us eight short years
How quickly the time did fly
We know he has a Master
Who is watching from on high.

Be a good boy Dear Jack
Like you used to listen
And come running gallantly
When you heard Don in the kitchen.

You had an appetite bar none
Even on a special diet
And when the doorbell rang
You never did keep quiet

So please Jack remember us
Keeping you more years was our plan
Seems life is more difficult
Since God took you to heaven.

OUR LAND

If you do not like America
Then go back from where you came
We will pledge our allegiance
Treasured like our famous name.

On national holidays we celebrate
With bands marching in our streets
Proudly presenting our colors
The red, white and blue can't be beat.

This is our country, we sing its praises
And by faith walk hand in hand
A great nation known for freedom
Whose culture long will stand.

With pride we behold liberty
And salute our Uncle Sam
You came and terrorized our country
It's time we make a plan.

To rid our shores from enemies
With all our power and might
May our leaders have the knowledge
Secure America without a fight.

OUR BELOVED JACK

Were I to knock on heaven's door
Would anyone let me in
My sins could be many
Where might I begin.

Maybe some are serious
Did confession take them away
If not I will keep asking
Daily when I pray.

Life has been kind and generous
Many days of tears and pain
I miss our Jack so very much
He filled each day with love again.

The master of all we do
Is written in the holy book
Loneliness is painful
In every place I look.

When people say I'm sorry
Some say it with a smile
But I wonder just how many
Lost a pet like our Jack.
He made my life worthwhile

He was our beloved Schnauzer
His coat smooth too our touch
After his bath each week
He was soft as a powder puff.

[OUR BELOVED JACK—continued]

We will get over being sad
About a wonderful pet we had
Maybe someday my tears will dry
And yet I ask myself why.

He loved everyone's gentle touch
Being up most days at five
Waiting for his daily walk
Happy being well and satisfied.

So happy just a few days before
What happened so suddenly
At five a.m. Sunday April Twenty-four
He left us alone, without a clue to me.

I could write a million pages
About the short eight years
Maybe someday I won't be lonely
Seems now all I do is shed tears.

Five long and lonely weeks
Have very slowly passed by
I wander around the house alone
Silently I cry.

I know the pain will never leave
People say get another
Life will never be the same
To Don and me he was our family
Like losing a dad or brother.

[OUR BELOVED JACK—continued]

When we meet again Dear Jack
We will build a throne
Where you will reign as king
Like you did at your number ten home.

Goodbye dear little pal
We sure miss your footstep patter
Loneliness still lingers
Tears fall as memories grow
To me it does not matter.

Jack you were a pal, buddy, friend
Lonesome are the days
You were someone to talk to
In many thousand ways.

HOPE

Have hope for someone lonely
By smile or clasp of hand
Make them feel they are needed
Somewhere in this glorious land.

Many feel what's the use
My job is hard labor
Stop and think of many
Even your next door neighbor.

I started work at age thirteen
Housecleaning for others
The necessity by reason
Having two sisters, five brothers.

So what do people do today
Gaining knowledge for success
Just sit at a desk pondering
What buttons do I press.

To offer, encourage a future
Few have this feeling I see
Not reaching out to help
This is the world of I, my and me.

CHELSEA

When you waken in the morning
Do you ever stop and say
I am thankful to be living
To greet another day.

Stop and think and wonder
How fast time will go
Pause a moment to recapture
What you did ten years ago.

I know you had a cat and dog
Bird and bunnies too
They multiplied rapidly
You had a rabbit zoo.

You also had another friend
You rode to many a show
He won you many ribbons
Your best friend Geronimo.

You are ready to graduate
High school days will end
Mom, dad and Callahan
Will always be your friend.

Mimi and poppa Clarke
Rick, Tim, Denny and Trish
Even though many miles apart
Call them if you wish.

[CHELSEA—continued]

When times get tough, studies rough
Through each day you live
Ask your guardian angel
Help when you forgive.

Go to church, God will hear
He knows when you feel sorrow
Walking with you every step
Today and each tomorrow.

Learning a serious business
Some days might not be sunny
Just call on me if needed
Try and save your money..

Your guardian angel
Watching everything you do
You never see her, never will
As duties you fulfill.

We used to see you often
Not so much anymore
Many things will upset you
Of this you can be sure.

Think you're ready for adult life
Forgive me when I say
Many times you will be lonesome
Happens to people everyday.

[CHELSEA—continued]

What the future holds for you
I wish you great success
Remember always many blessings
Will help in distress.

There are prayers for you
Want you to happy be
Ones you love are ever close
We are proud as can be.

Be careful on your journey
Off to college you go
Say your prayers
Stay healthy, safe and happy
Remembering we all love you so.

Love,

Grandma, May 2005

MY NAME

My name is Frances Kunzweiler
Not Irish never been
But when St Pat's Day rolls around
I'll be wearin' of the green.

A happy bunch of people
Every lass and laddie
Do not mess around with Irish jokes
Or you might irk their daddy.

Travel England, France or Germany
Or any place on earth, you'll find no snakes in Ireland
St. Pat chased them from the earth
Go sing an Irish tune with mirth.

So wearin' of the green like shamrocks
For St. Pat's Day celebrate
Corned beef 'n cabbage and taters
With an Irish pint by your plate.

IRELAND

An enchanted land of mystery
Bounded by the Irish Sea
The only one it's wonderful
Is Ireland golly gee.

Visiting there this was by choice
Not hard to understand
The kindness shown to one and all
The shake of an Irish hand.

Where we went and what we learned
Almost took one's breath away
The crystal and fine linens
Shopping for gifts everyday.

Oh yes we went to Galway
Visiting churches, heard choirs sing
The food was great, we stayed out late
As Irish pubs had everything.

One day the Ring of Kerry
Gave joy and happiness
A glass of Irish whisky
Put your tired body out of distress.

Some said it's foolish
To kiss the Blarney Stone
The magic of the Emerald Isle
Sure, like the shamrocks grown.

Watching them harvest potatoes
Or enjoying Irish tea

The fascination of children singing
Brought back young memories.

TWO THOUSAND FIVE

A new year is dawning
It's great to be alive
Two thousand four saw disasters
People suffered to survive.

The good Lord never gives us
More than we on earth can stand
Even folks are asking
What is happening in our land.

'tis people who cause problems
From homes in many places
An issue that bothers me
Are the children's small sad faces.

The USA known for freedom
We have help from few others
Sending troops to foreign countries
Who really are not known as brothers.

Please say prayers everyone
Serving across the nation
May come home to America
For a giant celebration.

RECALLING 1934

The old trunk I found
In the attic hidden away
Items wrapped with tender care
Held memories of yesterday.

A wedding dress of taffeta
Lined with finest lace
A pin of pearls and diamonds
Brought a smile to my face.

Picture of grandparents
Rested on a velvet chair
Smiles on faces of attendants
With ribboned hats of velvet
Adding charm to bouffant hair.

Old coins in a beaded bag
With draw strings to close it tight
As I proudly displayed all treasure
They were gazed on with delight.

Now at ninety years of age
I have memories of young and old
Never to trade with anyone
More precious to me than gold.

LONELY HALLS OF HELL

Not afraid of the enemy
Not afraid to die
Not afraid to be wishing
No more men must die
Tell me I'm lucky
Being home safe and well
They should know I can't forget
Those lonely halls of hell.

I roam around the country
Travel the best I can
Hitching a freight like a hobo
Don't know what to plan.
Yesterday's gone, today is here
Tomorrows never fail
Tired of roaming, time to rest
My story to unveil.

The way was long, my footsteps slow
Aching heart, head bent low
Roar of a plane, burst of a shell
Resounding through the halls of hell.
Being home is wonderful
Folks back here are swell
In still think of buddies
In the lonely halls of hell.

You wish me luck on my journeys
Saying may all go well

It's a safe return I'm hoping
For the soldiers in the halls of hell.

CALLAHAN

A single pound of energy
Add a smile wide as a mile
Mix with a lot of determination
Will make a day worthwhile.

My back aches, my head hurts
There is a pain in my toe
But even a bit of laughter
Is better than an inch of complaining you know.

With a cup of pep
Good thoughts by the dozen
Not for sale the wave of hand
A telephone call, a spoonful of pleasure
Is worth a hundred pounds of sand.

So let the good sense God gave you
Give you that ounce of inspiration
With a pinch of salt remember
A barrel of hope is the best foundation.

Practice, do you very best
At school and at home
Your mom, dad and Chelsea love you
Don't stray, stay and do not roam.

God will always help you
Whenever you feel distress
Watching every ball you pitch
With thoughts of years to bless.

Someday I hope to see you at bat
With a long hit home run

I pray that will come true
Before my life is done.

Love ya,

Grandma,

Cal

This little poem
Is all about
Someone I know
Always baseball playing
Never resting, always on the go
Why?
I would like to know
Find things tough
With everyone praying for you
Seldom see them smile
You are on the go
Never ever trying
To rest a while
You walk that extra mile
Well time is passing
Your life keeps moving on
I hope some will say
You made it
May heaven bless you everyone
Grandma asks and prays for you hope you do your best
Living, loving, learning to grow
Catch a second breath
Just walk along a lonely path
The hours quickly go
So do the years

Somewhere, sometime each day remember
Ask God to help you every day
From January to December.

ABCS OF LIFE

A is found in many words
An apple sure to please.
B found in butter
When you perform a task
If the burden seems heavy
Help will come if you only ask.
C a cuddly little creature
Your dog is called a pet
It will be a special friend
Causes no need to fret.
D do don't dare or care
When you feel in a fog
A pal you love forever
Your precious Schnauzer dog.
E effort many times difficult
If the going gets too rough
Trust in your perfection
Finding the answer is enough
F found in family
Stay close keep them around
If they start to wander
Prayer will bring them homeward bound..
G great world for searching peace
Of which we are a part
Like grandparents everywhere
Helping grandchildren get a start.

H happiness, hope, heaven
Times you feel distress
Use one of these words to assist you
It might help you to progress.
I imagination, conversation
In this life you live
Never cause aggravation
God will help you to forgive.
J found in joy, joke jealousy
Some happy or contrite
Only one gives much pleasure
It is joy that brings delight.
K being kind a simple thing
Shown by all you meet
We show everyone kindness
At home all along the street.
L love, life, liberty
Surrounds each every day
Loneliness will disappear
When happiness comes to stay.
M memories surpass anxiety
Think of yesteryear
Hold these close forever
Happiness is always near.
N never let a day go by
Find a task to keep busy
Climb the ladder of enchantment
Rather than get in a nervous tizzy.

O I see in cooperation
Also in isolation located in a nation
Then log on to information.
P pause a moment do not refuse
Using words for publication
Find them in your daily news
You learned on your vacation.
Q question not what someone's doing
A busy mind has something brewing
Search for answers you might find
They will give you peace of mind.
R ready, rough, real, reply
Perhaps some might ask why
Show each day you begin
Causes ideas when you grin.
S summer, sunshine flowers bloom
Vacation time is coming soon
Sailing, swimming lots of fun
Keeping families on the run.
T time to stop and ponder
Thoughts make one wonder
Share laughter forget sorrow
Hope for better times tomorrow.
U uselessness a strong word
Seldom spoken, seldom heard
Help someone a fault to mend
Peace inside will never end.

[ABCS OF LIFE—continued]

V visions of a place to travel
Let your problems unravel
Think of Venus also Mars
Golden moon sky full of stars.
W who, what, where, when, why
Questions asked through the years
Each of them have an answer
But "why" often causes tears.
XYZ three left of the alphabet
Don't be anxious do not fret
Young folks never realize
They zoom to live beyond their size.

GENTLE RAIN

Having a dream quite often
Places visited and sites seen
Takes me back to yesteryear
Life seemed more quiet, more serene.

Everyone today is busy
Time passes rapidly they say
They should save effort for tomorrow
E'en a minute out to pray

Pay someone a little visit
You haven't seen for a while
If they should feel down hearted
Share a joke, make them smile.

You know thunder and lightning
Rains fall making all things gleam
Seems a miracle from heaven
Turning lawns to emerald green.

Awaken to the wonder
Dreams you had before
Those are memories
Gone as days of yore.

If you reach out a friendly hand
Helping someone bear their loss
Life will never be as heavy
As God carrying his cross.

STEPHANIE

I need to write a story
About a little girl I used to see
She was busy and loving
Always happy and carefree.

Growing up so rapidly
The oldest great grandchild of four
With Joe, Chelsea and Callahan
No one could ask for more.

They each were educated
By loving parents
Did very well I'm told
Never thinking of getting old.

With things or stories
They might tell you see
This one I'm writing about
Her name *Stephanie.*

No more idle hours
Now busy as a bee
With two of her own
One for rocking on each knee.

Chase is the master
Really likes going to school
And can help Maddison
When she's old enough to rule.

Grandma, December 2006

CHRISTMAS 2006

The Christmas Poinsettia
Leaves that turn scarlet
When the last months
Arrive fill my heart
With happiness praying
God is on our side
Faithful know he's
Watching over us
On this earth
As soon we celebrate
The magnificent time
Of his birth
In church, choirs
Will be singing
Celebrating everywhere
Children will be waiting
For Santa to appear
I do not wish
For gifts or money
To me life is grand
It was more than ninety
Years ago I was born
In this great land
Living loving learning
Writing poetry through the ages
Hoping someone somewhere
Will enjoy the pages.
Folks search for treasure
Take some time for pleasure
And someone who's needy

Will have a memory
To measure
As the red poinsettia
Brought a smile to all on earth
The almighty will
Fill our stocking
On the eve of his birth
Soon we will say goodbye
To twenty—o—six
Turn the page to twenty-o-seven
In this great land
To fill our hearts with mirth.

IN 1927

I left the farm where I lived
The year II was just thirteen
Went to Springfield to work
making five dollars a week
was like living in a dream.

Gave my mom two dollars
Enough to buy a few extra things
My five brothers got a quarter each
Which would buy next to nothing.

Doing housework in people's homes
Washing, ironing, windows, scrubbing floors
Helping neighbors in their gardens
Gave me a quarter for my chores.

On Saturday or some weekday
I'd visit bressmer's department store
Met someone I called aunt teen
Those memories long endure.

DREAMS

Dreaming I was on a mission
Moving extra slow
Woke up trying for an answer
Reached a blank, will never know.

I was carrying roses
To someone with a smile
Accepting them gave pleasure
Ask, may I walk with you awhile.

Stars were shining brightest
Moon was like a golden dollar
We strolled along Ormond beach
Holding schnauzer jack by his collar.

That someone was my angel
She is always at my side
Oft times wondering in reality
Was she sent by God to guide.

My prayer is a thank you
Each hour of the day
Peace of mind I will find
Remembering dreams won't fade away.

JOHN-JOHN

Your sister is all alone now John
She needed you so much
But God will stand beside her
And give her life a special touch.

The world still ponders how
We stood those tragedies so long
Is it because God gives his greatest love
To the children who are strong.

Your father thought for certain
His mantel you would wear
Because his blood flowed through your veins
His dreams you would bring to bear

Everyone could see it unfolding
It was a perfect plan
Somehow that was not to be
Those earthly plans of man.

Standing tall about the rest
And never looking down
You always walked beside them
Where life and love abound.

The family mourns your passing John
It's hard for all to see
Why you were taken from us
We ask, how could this be?

You were the prince of Camelot
As being next in line

Plans and expectations were
For you to test the wine.

The world is very saddened
Their grief is shown with pain
Mourn not only who you were
And what you could have been.

I pray you will remember
As the days pass into years
You loved your wife and life on earth
With laughter, hope and tears.

Please God take care of Caroline
Give her peace, space, let her be
The person that she chooses
Will you please do that
For dad and mom and me.

We are not their to shield her
Protecting her from all harm
That often comes to sisters
A lovely lady full of charm.

I QUIT

My fingers are tired, my back is pained
My mind is weary; it's been a strain
Getting together these poems
Written through the years
Many folded and faded
Some have disappeared.

Pleasures they bring
As I read aloud
About many people
Of whom I am proud
Who added so much
Down through the ages
Memories return
As I read the pages.

It gave me cause
To add charm and wit
To the written articles
So now, I quit.

978-0-595-43661-3
0-595-43661-7

Printed in the United States
75181LV00004B/115-138

9 780595 436613